On the Run in America

Or...Crime for Free

Jacob Monroe

Intro

On August 30, 2020, the Mayor of Chicago defended her right to safety after requesting police to keep her neighborhood free of protesters and rioters. The Mayor proclaimed her right to protection from those who may threaten her or her family.

Believing that protesters should never have the right to gather outside someone's own home to threaten or create a disturbance, I agree with the Mayor. The act of protesting and gathering outside a person's house is nothing more than an attempt to create fear for those within. It is a tactic based on hate and potential violence to silence free speech and scare the opposition. This type of demonstration should have no rightful place in a free American society. When protestors corral others in their home with a potentially dangerous confrontation to impose their will on those they hate, they have gone beyond their right to freedom. By denying others safety and protection under the law, the rioters have become criminals.

However, while the Mayor now resides in the safety of her own home, Chicago burns.

While the Mayor is safely tucked away in her house, her entire block protected with a barrier of police; other neighborhoods watch as innocent children are gunned down. While dancing for mom in the living room or doing homework upstairs, children are nothing more than collateral damage. At the same time, gangs, drug dealers, and criminals hold neighborhoods in the grip of fear with the threat of death.

While the Mayor claims the right to safety with a police wall protecting her community, downtown Chicago is taken over by criminal thugs. They are looting and burning their way to profitability, at the expense of Chicago's business owners. These riots have nothing to do with Justice. Injustice does not bring about Justice. These individuals on the streets, filled with hate and madness, are destroying and threatening all who oppose them. However, at least, the Mayor is safe.

Many will claim that these riots are an offshoot of the death of George Floyd. However, one B.L.M. rioter stated that the looting and burning were simply reparations. Rioters are just taking what is theirs. The insurance companies will pay off the businesses anyway. From designer sweaters to toys for tots, the rioters, and looters, who burn and threaten anyone in their way, are just reclaiming what belongs to them. This is the criminal thought process at its finest.

Media enjoys espousing the idea that those on the streets who riot, loot, and burn are justly upset. These rioters responsible for the murders of more than a few black men themselves are angry over police brutality. These men and women filled with hate and violence are seeking Justice. Even as they loot and burn down the businesses of black men and women in Minneapolis, who worked hard to support their families, the rioters' claim Black Lives Matter.

And across America, in the cities where riots and violence are erupting nightly, the rioter's hatred and cruel makeup did not begin with the death of George Floyd. Many of these rioters were already criminals, nurtured in the bail reform movement adopted by the communities where these riots are raging.

Before the death of George Floyd, across America, where bail reform has taken hold, crime and violence soared. New York crime is out of control. Seattle, Portland, and Chicago all nurtured their criminals, assuring them of freedom without accountability. San Francisco has become a Property Crime Capital.

In every city where nighttime rioting, looting, and burning take place, bail reform arrived first. Bail Reform allowed criminal suspects the right to freedom without accountability, without fear of jail. They were comforted as the victims of their own crimes.

Bail Reform nurtured criminal suspects and helped them grow into full-fledged violent and dangerous individuals. Bail Reform encouraged a Crime for Free mentality where individuals engaged in breaking the law can roam the streets and cross state lines without fear of capture or penalties. In this atmosphere of bail-reform-compassion, arrogance, and a new sense of criminal entitlement have grown.

George Floyd was simply their excuse to do what was already in their heart. The hatred and violence they display nightly, their disrespect for others, and their self-empowerment to drag innocent people onto the streets for beatings were not a flash-moment of self-discovery. Their belief in the right to threaten others, demand and destroy whatever pleases them did not overtake them one morning while eating a bowl of cheerios.

Their current criminal entitlement state reflects a learning process that began and was years in the making, which bail reform encouraged. It is not always conscious learning, but experience is still a great teacher.

The accused who dragged out an innocent man to beat him half to death while the crowd cheered was not a man upset over the death of George Floyd. His criminal life, his hatred, and violence began long before. As with many of the rioters, his crazed, violent actions are no more than the freeing his inner self, encouraged by politicians on the sideline and a willing press. But it did not begin here and now.

George Floyd was their excuse, not their cause.

Those who walked the streets in peaceful protests were inspired to speak against police brutality. And where police are out of control, Justice is required. However, injustice does not create truth.

The riots are only a result of a process that began in hearts of hate, nourished along, and encouraged by life's lessons. One of those lessons was Bail Reform.

The cities where these riots flare up nightly is the evidence presented. Each city already had a crime problem. These cities each took part in the bail reform movement, where the criminals were the victims and only required compassion and understanding. All these municipalities bought into the Crime for Free process of bail reform. These cities also now enjoy the fruit of their change, with high crime rates, violence, disrespect, lawless arrogance, and their downtowns a virtual criminal enterprise.

A question asked by a reporter in Chicago explains the result of bail reform clearly. The reporter was questioning Chicago's Police Superintendent on the cause of the ongoing riots. *It almost sounds as though you were saying – the reason we have this is the courts and the prosecutors were not doing their jobs, that they were going too easy on the looters from the last time around.*

Don't take it from me, Superintendent Brown replied. *Just go about what's been done. There were no consequences for the people arrested.*

It was then that the Mayor, risking life and limb by emerging from the safety of her police protected enclave, stepped up to the mike. **Do not bait us,** she stated with defiance.

However, before no consequences, were the bail reform statutes in Chicago that gave quick freedom to the arrested rioters. Bail reform enabled them to run back to their favorite store before somebody else looted all the good stuff. After their Crime for Free release, they were free to roam about the burning fires and fulfill their criminal fantasies without fear of prosecution. And rather than explain or answer tough questions regarding a cause, **'Don't bait us,'** was a clean, quick Mayoral response that could ignore the issue.

Freeing criminal suspects without accountability, allowing fugitives to roam the countryside without fear of prosecution, are all fruits of bail reform. And it is the one word that is never mentioned in bail reform that screams in the night. That word is the word Victim. And there will be more victims, and their names and their lives will mean little to those pushing the reform that, according to one former governor, has been devastating to her state's citizens.

Minneapolis now showcases the end game of bail reform by demanding the defunding of the police, as rioters burn down and loot businesses because a suspect murderer committed suicide.

As reported by the New York Post on August 27, 2020, a murder suspect being cornered by the police committed suicide. The officers on the scene never even drew a weapon. However, the murder suspect, feeling cornered, shot himself dead. Then in less than two hours, the ever-ready righteous rioters and looters hit the streets once more. Their cause was that of murder. De-fund the police means to ***De-Fund the Police***. Leave our murderers alone!

After boring of their peaceful protest demanding justice for the dead accused murderer, these protesters began their nightly shopping spree, breaking storefront windows and looting. However, rather than burning out the businesses of hard-working black women and men, at least this time, they hit Saks Fifth Ave on Nicollet Mall. Now they can dress up for their next riot!

The demonstrators were told the suspect killed himself, and the police quickly released a video to show they were not involved with his death. However, demonstrators did not care. Naturally, it was still the fault of the police. What gives police the right to track down a murder suspect anyway? Allow people to rule themselves with vigilante mob insanity, inspired by hate and violence. Let the rioter's rule.

Did any concerned Minneapolis citizens walk the streets to demonstrate against murderers? Were any of the rioters looting stores on behalf of the man killed by the murder suspect? In the **Bail Reform Movement** and follow up, **De-fund the Police** push, the victims of crime have no value. It is those who commit crimes who are cherished and empowered.

From bail reform to defunding the police, Minneapolis is a painting of the future. Murderers are idolized, and violence the daily mandate.

Jacob

Chapters

On the Run in America

Chapter 1. A Family of Fugitives - Accountability
A True Story -

This is not the movie *National Lampoon's American Family Vacation* starring Chevy Chase.

This is a tale of fraud, theft, drugs, and bad checks; a family of fugitives criming and drugging their way across America, State by State. And they were not going to Disneyland.

The trip began in Florida, where the mother, a felon needing to escape outstanding warrants for fraud, possession of a firearm, and parole violations, decided to travel west. Her husband went with her.

The woman's daughter, who had her own felony warrant out of Florida for fraud and her 19-year-old brother, accompanied their parents on this incredible American journey westward.

They made one stop in Texas on their trip west, where a second daughter had a seven-year-old. This daughter was in such a drugged-up state; the criminal family caravan appeared to be a better and safer alternative than the daughter's own drug-addled efforts to care for her little girl.

And so, the family of four became a family of five.

In Colorado, the family found a nook that seemed safe, and they set up shop. However, it was here that the father added to the family's criminal history by catching multiple arrests for drug possession and driving under the influence. When he still could not follow the rules, he picked up a probation violation. The maternal criminal maître d' was then arrested on her outstanding Florida warrant.

Also, their son found himself in jail after being caught and charged with drug possession. Only the daughter, wanted in Florida for fraud, eluded arrest in Colorado.

Following their slew of new arrests, after obtaining their release once more, the family's lives became a calendar of court dates.

Their seven-year-old grandchild? She also had a scheduled day in court. However, her court hearing did not involve a criminal act she had committed. Her court hearing included the Colorado D.H.S. (Department of Human Services) after department personnel became concerned that the grand daughter's living environment was not secure. Her D.H.S. hearing required her and her grandparents to appear in court to show proof she was safe while in their custody. Their arrests, drug usage, and lifestyle were flagged as risk factors, endangering the child's life.

At this point, the family had a sit-down and decided Colorado was no longer the beautiful, welcoming paradise they had first envisioned. They concluded their best avenue of dealing with the multiple criminal cases against them, and the risk of losing their granddaughter was to pack their bags and head further west. Although their flight from Colorado would initiate more arrest warrants, they had little concern anyone would come after them.

Three of the four family members obtained their releases through various state-run Pretrial release programs. Florida released the daughter on her own special Pretrial release and the dad and son through Colorado's Pretrial release. The family knew that once they crossed the state line, they would have no fears. No one would spend time or money trying to track them down. A state-run Pretrial service doesn't work that way.

As for the Mother—the criminal maître d'—she had to use a bail bond agent to help her post her $20,000 bond for her Florida "fugitive from justice" charge. Now, if she failed to appear in court, the bail bond agent would have to locate her, arrest her, then return her to jail or lose $20,000. Of course, the mother did not care about what a bail agent might lose and did not believe the agent would send anyone after her.

A bail bond is a monetary amount pledged to a court by a defendant or another third party who promises the Defendant will appear in court when the court requires it. If the Defendant fails to appear in court, the court can demand payment of the bond amount. It is a system of accountability that has existed in some form since the days of the Roman Empire. If the Defendant goes to court, he or she never pays the bond. If the Defendant fails to appear in court, there is a risk of financial loss.

Government-run Pretrial Services programs screen those arrested and offer to release them without a financial requirement. It is a system based on what one person believes and another agrees to. One thinks the other will go to court, the other promises to go, and the criminal suspect is released.

The problem of using a government-run pre-trial system for freeing criminal suspects is that, when it becomes the lone operating principle for release, there is no accountability. Without accountability, the operation is nothing more than a hope that a criminal suspect who promises to appear in court will show.

Where commercial bail bond agents operate, there *is* accountability. Each time a bond is posted to free a criminal suspect, the bail bonding agent that posted the bond becomes accountable for the Defendant's appearance in court.

If a defendant on a commercial bond fails to appear in court, it is the bail-bonding agent's responsibility to locate, arrest, and return the criminal suspect to jail. If they fail to find and capture the Defendant, the agent is liable to pay to the court the entire amount of the bond posted. It is a means of accountability assuring a court that the Defendant will appear or that someone will be held responsible for the Defendant's non-appearance.

The three adult fugitives facing charges in Colorado decided that if they were not going to appear in court on their criminal cases, then there was really no need to appear in court for their granddaughter's custody hearings, either. Taking hold of the little girl's hand, they embarked on her first run from Justice.

However, before they fled Colorado, the criminal family's maître d' and her husband stole blank company checks and a company credit card from their employer. While making their escape, traveling Northwest from Colorado to Idaho, then Oregon, they used an app on their phone and electronically cashed these checks through a company in Florida. Their scam netted them $3,000. Flush in cash, they had enough money to find a safe house and resettle under new aliases.

That was about when the bail bonding agent who had posted the $20,000 bond for the female ringleader contracted with a fugitive recovery agent. The recovery agent was asked to find the fugitive, who had failed to appear in court. If he did not locate her, the court would require the bail agent to pay the defendant's $20,000 bond.

While tracking this Grandmother of Crime, the fugitive recovery agent received information that her daughter was still in Colorado in the Buena Vista area. The agent attempted to make contact, but the daughter had no interest in that contact, and after several weeks of remaining out of sight, she and her boyfriend also fled Colorado for the Northwest.

A family of fugitives, *On the Run in America.*

This family was a crime-wise, streetwise group. They had been in the system for many years and would not be easy to track. It took two months of street-time investigations and many hours

by the fugitive recovery agent's researcher to get a line on where this family may have settled.

On their way to the Northwest, this family attempted to use a credit card belonging to their previous employer. The credit card was rejected, but the attempted use was a directional signal. The fugitives had had better fortune with the stolen checks, and their Colorado employer lost thousands. Still, the employer was hesitant to file charges.

A dilemma for investigators tracking fugitives in America are the misguided individuals who believe covering for those on the run is a good and right course of action. Families will not supply information. Friends won't speak out. Even, it seems, some states protect fugitives. These criminal suspects, who are arrested for a crime and released from jail on their promise to appear in court, often do not feel like keeping that promise. Instead of showing up for their court date, they show up in a new state under the care of everyone who aided their run.

The people, whether family members, friends, and even the states that prevent their capture and return to face justice, aid and abet these fugitives on their run, allowing them the freedom to prey on others and commit new crimes, *criming* their way from State to State.

While on the run, criminal suspects have a high propensity for committing additional crimes, putting innocent people in danger, and creating new victims. Many fugitives operate freely, having no fear they will ever be arrested on their old warrants and returned to the State that issued it. Unless they obtain their freedom by posting a commercial bail bond, they know no one is looking for them.

These individuals—jailed for an array of crimes from D.U.I.'s and domestic violence to drugs, thefts, and robberies—who gain their freedom via a state-run Pretrial release, have already been schooled on the premise that crossing the state line is their ticket to freedom.

With commercial bail, each bail-bonding agent is accountable to the court that holds the bond. Because they are responsible, they will actively pursue these fugitives, or they will contract with professional fugitive recovery agents to do the same. A bail bondsman does not allow a state line to stop them from pursuing a fugitive.

When operating as the sole principle of release from jail, government-run Pretrial Programs are considered by many as no more than **Crime-for-Free Programs**. Pretrial Service's operational blueprint gave it its nickname: Crime For Free. Government-run Pretrial Release programs release prisoners without any accountability or responsibility to guarantee a defendant's court appearance. Pretrial agents have no obligation to assure anyone that the Defendant will appear in court. If the Defendant fails to appear in court, Pretrial is not responsible for locating, arresting, or returning these defendants to jail. It is a **Crime-for-Free bond**. You commit the crime, get arrested, and we'll free you.

For those individuals who break their promise to appear in court and thereby avoid prosecution, simply crossing one or two state boundaries often assures them of freedom, untouched by the arms of the law.

Many times, the State the runner flees from will not pursue the fugitive who escapes their jurisdictional coverage. Once across that magical state line, other jurisdictions have no legal authority to arrest the offender if no extraditable warrant is issued.

Each State has what is called an extraditable schedule. This schedule outlines the crimes that will qualify a fugitive for an extraditable warrant. The list of crimes earning these warrants varies based on each State's financial position and interests. By assessing the costs and interest level for prosecution, the State creates an extraditable tier system that allows many fugitives to go on the run without any fear of extradition, even when caught. This schedule enables a prosecutor's office to pursue those who they consider the most severe and dangerous offenders without going broke.

The problem with attempting to determine which criminals are dangerous and not is often no more than a guessing game. The purpose of commercial bail is to allow for the protection of the justice system by giving the bail-bonding agent an incentive to ensure that the arrestee appears in court between hearings after their release from jail on a bond. This incentive assures the bail-bonding agent will act in the justice system's best interest by being accountable to the justice system they serve.

What needs to be clear at this point is that a court has the power to issue an extraditable warrant in any case if a defendant fails to appear in court. A judge can order an extraditable warrant for either a misdemeanor or a felony. However, if issued, the local sheriff's department will be left to enter the national crime computer's extraditable warrant. A few Colorado sheriffs refuse to place a fugitive's name into the national database if the crime and the extradition are of no interest to them.

When an extraditable warrant *is* issued and entered into the national crime database, and the fugitive caught, the district attorney's office will decide on whether to pursue the return of the individual wanted. If the district attorney involved is not interested in the extradition, the fugitive is never returned and is released and free to start again.

Why does law enforcement refuse to extradite criminals on misdemeanor and lower-class felonies once these same suspects leave the State?

1. Money: The cost of extradition is not cheap. The process can be long and cumbersome, requiring time and commitment that is needed elsewhere. Extraditing every criminal that flees could bankrupt a State.
2. A district attorney does not wish to bother with the fugitive. The fugitive is out of the State. Good riddance. Let them bother someone else. Let the new state deal with the results and acts of this fugitive now living among their citizenries.
3. As in a few Colorado cases and across the country, county sheriffs do not care about the fugitive's return. There are times when a sheriff may choose not to enter select fugitive information into the national crime database, even when the court orders an extraditable warrant.

Arresting a fugitive and returning them to face Justice ensures that Justice and gives life to the hope of Justice for the victim as well. The fugitive's return strengthens the criminal justice system by securing the continuation of that system.

A fugitive's removal from the streets also often prevents a new victim and a new crime. While on the run, most suspects continue engaging in criminal acts. Having escaped the consequences of their actions by leaving the State that issued their warrant, they have no reason to change; what has worked for them in the past will serve them well in the future.

It is unfortunate that when a fugitive is on the run in many cases, a victim is left with the pain of the fugitive's destruction, while a potential new victim waits in the wings. The victim they discard in the wake of their crime is victimized once more, as they suffer alone with their injuries or losses. The new victim awaits in innocence, unaware that soon they may also suffer at the hands of one who disregards others' laws and rights, one who holds contempt for the justice system: a justice system set up to ensure those rights.

When a fugitive goes on the run, the criminal determines that they can do what they want, to anyone they want, whenever they want. An offender claims their rights by denying everyone else theirs, including the right to Justice.

A fugitive's attitude of flipping off the justice system is a dangerous one that consistently threatens society's safety and well-being. A criminal suspect on the loose endangers every new innocent individual the fugitive will encounter next. Their run from the law undermines the very justice system designed to uphold the law.

A reporter at *U.S.A. Today*, Brad Heath completed an extensive study on the issue of fugitives on the run. He reported that even offenders released on minor charges, who run, later can commit horrid crimes. In ***"The Fugitive Next Door"*** and ***"The Ones That Get Away,"*** Heath clearly outlined the prolific growth in the number of fugitives running across state lines and the growing number of states that refuse to have them returned to face their crimes.

In one article, Heath reports a minimum of 186,000 felony fugitives running around with no fear of suffering the consequences of their crimes. That would also mean there are close to 180,000 victims left in these fugitives' wakes because these fugitives have decided they need not answer to anyone. These are victims who will never see justice for the crimes committed against them.

It also means that there are, at any given moment, 186,000 innocent individuals who have the potential of becoming the fugitive's next victim. A fugitive on the run seldom has the opportunity or, for that matter, any reason to change, alter their behavior, or find honest work. ***These fugitives can continue to take advantage of others who do not suspect or know that a criminal has targeted them while on the run.***

If there are 180,000 fugitives on the run with felony warrants, there are three times that number running from misdemeanor warrants. These fugitives, mistakenly overlooked after they run, are wanted for crimes considered minor crimes not worth pursuing.

When one thinks of a misdemeanor as a minor crime, one is downgrading domestic violence's seriousness. A domestic violence charge will not be a petty crime for the woman next up on this fugitive's date card. This fugitive's offense is also not an unimportant crime to the victim left in their wake once they decide to go on the run to avoid prosecution, to avoid facing up to their actions, to avoid changing.

When T.V. cameras are rolling, domestic violence has prime-time importance. However, once the accused flees the State, their case appears to be no more than a minor inconvenience for most everyone but their victims.

First, second, and third D.U.I. Offenses are non-extraditable, minor crimes. They are front-page crimes when the State Patrol does a media blitz regarding D.U.I. Enforcement and taking these potential killers off the road. But once released from jail, if they drive across the state line, their crime is no longer significant. No T.V. cameras or political speeches will follow these fugitives on the run, no media blitz about the potential dangers they now pose to innocent individuals.

However, a family of four on their way home from a night out, broadsided by a drunk driver on the run from another state, may not find this fugitive's offense or warrant a minor one. The survivors from a horrific accident involving a drunk driver fleeing another state may not understand why the offender was not arrested and returned to custody before they could cause even more harm. They may wonder why no one else cared enough to force this driver to face the consequences of their previous actions, enforcement that may have saved the life of one or more innocent individuals.

Regarding the fugitive family that fled Colorado, criming their way to Oregon, the families' criminal maître d' did not obtain her freedom from a state-run Pretrial operation. The Florida fugitive, mother of two, grandmother of one, did not post a bond through a Pretrial *Crime-for-Free* program. She had to use a private bonding agent, allowing that bail-bonding agent the option to pursue.

Commercial bail-bonding agents in Colorado do have accountability and do not allow their defendants to run free. When a bail-bonding agent can locate a fugitive for whom they posted a bond, they *will* act. Either they will arrest and return the wanted criminal themselves, or they will hire a fugitive recovery agent to do it.

After a couple of months, the fugitive recovery agent working the case of the Colorado fugitive family developed what he believed was a viable lead. He packed his bags and left for Ontario, Oregon. He had no address or specific worksite provided, just a hint that this family might be in Ontario, Oregon. However, the tip carried with it enough probability that the trip itself was worth the gamble and the cost.

Since Ontario, Oregon was a small city bordering Idaho; this trip could have involved a two-state search. Many criminal suspects on the run research and seek out states friendly to fugitives. These states aid and abet the wanted by banning bail-bonding or fugitive recovery agents from operating within their borders to capture and return these same criminals.

Oregon appeared to prohibit the capture and removal of any fugitive by a bail-bonding or fugitive recovery agent. Although this could pose a problem, locating the offender was the priority. There was no law preventing a fugitive recovery agent from locating a fugitive, even in Oregon. Whether or not the agent could make the arrest was another matter entirely.

For the fugitive recovery agent, Ontario, Oregon appeared to be a small city where locating a family of fugitives should not be difficult. He did not know his easy task would take him twelve days.

The agent spotted the daughter's vehicle on day two of his arrival in Ontario. However, tailing this daughter from a Walmart parking lot would prove more complicated than a T.V. show. Both the daughter and her boyfriend were pros at counter-surveillance.

On television, a detective or a police officer can pull in behind the target and tail them along deserted streets, down alleys, and across town, without ever being noticed. The criminal never realizes that the vehicle directly behind them the entire time is following them. It just does not occur to them that anyone would want to tail them. In real life, however, individuals on the run often have a sixth sense. They watch for tails; they look for anyone who might be looking for them.

In this case, the daughter of the fugitive this recovery agent was chasing remained vigilant, always on the lookout. She and her boyfriend would circle the Walmart parking lot, park, look around, pull out and reverse their circle, stopping again to see if anyone appeared a little too interested in their movement. Another trick they employed was driving toward an exit as if to leave, then turning off at the last minute. They would then watch the cars that had been behind them for any erratic maneuver made.

A perfect-picture situation can take up to five vehicles to successfully track and follow a target vehicle without being noticed. The fugitive recovery agent in this pursuit only had one car. It did not take the daughter long to figure out she was being tailed and wonder who was trying to follow her.

Before the Oregon trip, the fugitive recovery agent had his vehicle crushed by a rental truck on a Colorado mountain pass. The truck had switched lanes to prevent one accident, only to cause another. For this reason, the agent had picked up a rental car. This rental had worked out fortuitously, though, as the rental vehicle's Missouri license plates became a form of vehicle disguise, camouflaging the agent's intent.

The mommy fugitive had jumped bond in Colorado. Her family had run with her from Colorado. If someone were coming for them, the family would have assumed that person or persons would be driving a vehicle with Colorado plates. The Missouri plates stumped them and allowed the fugitive recovery agent a little more leeway and freedom to maneuver around town without gaining their immediate suspicion.

Oregon is one of the few states that, at a distance, appear to protect their fugitives. When a criminal on the run flees to Oregon, the Oregon state statutes do not allow a fugitive recovery agent or investigator to arrest and remove that fugitive from the State and return them to the location where their warrant waits. Oregon does not have commercial bail. For this reason, they are a favorite state for fugitives seeking refuge.

Many a criminal in Washington State, a state with commercial bail, cross the state line into Oregon to make their escape. In Oregon, they feel safe knowing the bail-bonding agent, fugitive recovery agent, or anyone else will be prevented from effecting their arrest and returning them to face Justice. It is the proverbial fugitive game of hide-and-seek. Except that in Oregon and a few other states, fugitives can hide in plain sight. In their flight from Justice, it can sometimes be the State they run to that aids and abets them.

Fortunately, regarding the female fugitive from Colorado, the agent discovered several Oregon State laws that could work to his benefit. Oregon statutes appeared to allow a bail-bonding

agent or fugitive recovery agent the right to arrest a fugitive if the charges accompanying the warrant carried a potential sentence of over a year in prison. The family's maître d' of crime had also breached a security release when she'd fled Colorado, an arrestable crime in Oregon.

And now, somebody reported her to be hiding out in a trailer park in or around Ontario. The fugitive recovery agent began a grid search to locate the fugitive's lair. One trailer park at a time.

When the agent wasn't attempting to locate the fugitive's residence, he played cat and mouse with the fugitive's daughter and her boyfriend, who seemed to have an affinity for Walmart parking lots. On the sixth day, the agent was finally able to follow their vehicle long enough to cut his search grid in half.

Although spotting the daughter was a valuable confirmation that the mom was close by, the daughter's own Florida warrant for fraud was not extraditable. She was out on a Pretrial *Crime-for-Free* bond. After her arrest for fraud, she had promised she would appear in court. However, once she was released, she changed her mind, and no one cared. No one was going to come for her, and she knew it. The recovery agent's job was to locate and arrest the mom. For this reason, he had to be incredibly careful not to spook the daughter until he found the mom.

Although the agent did have information that the mother could be working at a local hotel, the exact hotel was unknown. Also, approaching the various hotels and motels openly, asking questions, and showing the fugitive's picture, could prove a dangerous move. The criminal could catch wind of her impending arrest before her capture. In unknown surroundings, one needs to be careful whom they question. Talking with anyone is a risk. Would a hotel clerk or maid lead an agent astray and tip off the fugitive? Trusting anyone on an investigation is a gamble.

And so, the days wore on as the recovery agent marked off trailer park after trailer park in the evening and staked out hotels and motels early in the morning.

At one point, the agent attempted to enlist the help of the local Ontario Police. Their interest amounted to a weak promise that they would keep an eye out. To the recovery agent, this meant that if his fugitive walked up to them, introduced herself, and informed the police she was wanted, they *might* arrest her. Other than that, they did not appear to care.

Finally, after constant persistence, as the agent drove through one trailer park campground several miles east of Ontario, he spotted the daughter's vehicle parked at a small trailer home. The trailer park had approximately thirteen trailers, so the agent was sure everyone knew everyone. However, even though he spotted the daughter's vehicle, he did not see the Colorado Chevrolet Tahoe the mom had fled in. He had to be careful and so put the trailer park on hold, returning to his temporary hangout, a rest stop off the highway, to review his next move and relax in the fresh breeze of a quiet afternoon.

The next afternoon as he staked out a motel he believed the fugitive mom might be working at, the daughter and boyfriend drove by in front of him, turned into the suspect motel, then made a U-turn and pulled alongside the agent. The agent turned his attention to his phone to defer their suspicion. They cruised by ever so slowly and into another parking lot. He knew he had been made and left the area.

At this point, the agent feared the streetwise fugitives might bolt. They knew the agent had appeared to focus his interest directly on them. Needing to throw off their suspicion, the agent had to come up with a plan.

Every investigation has a plan of operation. However, it never takes long for these planned-out operational guidelines to fall apart. When they do, the situation becomes fluid, requiring an active imagination. Ideas generated on the fly have captured more than their fair share of fugitives.

In this case, the fugitive recovery agent decided to go online and pull up Missouri's Most Wanted. After selecting one, he printed out the mug shot, bought a throw-away phone with a Missouri number, and made a wanted poster featuring one of Missouri's Most Wanted.

On the wanted poster, the agent described the Missouri fugitive's vehicle as a blazer that was similar in appearance to the S.U.V. the fugitive daughter had been driving around. The agent then took his wanted posters to the trailer park, where he had previously spotted the daughter's vehicle.

As he pulled into the park, the daughter and her boyfriend pulled out, driving right by the agent on the small dirt road that led to the park. The situation was getting heated.

Once in the trailer park, the agent gathered his newly printed wanted posters and passed them out door to door. The agent also made a point to talk with several individuals living at the park, explaining that he had been chasing this Missouri fugitive for months and had gotten a tip the culprit was living in a campground or trailer park close to Ontario, Oregon. He was hoping to complete the masquerade with his Missouri plates and hold off any suspicions long enough to get an exact fix on the real target of his investigation: the fugitive mom.

As he walked through the park, playing his role, he came to an empty trailer. Next to the trailer sat a dark gray Chevrolet Tahoe, the exact make and model the fugitive mom had fled in. Containing his excitement, he circled to spy the vehicle's license plate and caught a view of the Colorado Mountains: green mountains that signified a Colorado Plate.

The agent walked to the door of a residence adjacent to the Tahoe. As he folded a flyer to place on the door, he heard the distinct sound of a little girl and an older man talking. The agent immediately felt a surge of adrenalin. In his gut, he knew he had discovered his target's safe house. Placing the flyer on the door, the agent turned and left, memorizing the Tahoe's plate number.

Once he had driven out of the trailer park, the agent contemplated his next step. He knew that the two men accompanying the fugitive mom, both the husband and the son, had a propensity for violence and enjoyed playing with knives. Without the typical authority and ability to arrange a team to hit the trailer, the agent's options were limited. The game of tracking and securing a fugitive's arrest is not all bravado; being mindful of safety and timing when getting a runner off the streets limits risk to all.

The fugitive recovery agent had his researcher in Colorado run the plate number. It came back a solid hit, registered to the fugitive mother of crime, under one of her aliases.

The agent drove back into Ontario. It was Friday night, and no one who could help was around. County Law enforcement offices were closed over the weekend, and they would not respond unless one called 911. The agent called the Florida Sheriff's Office, where the fugitive mom's extraditable warrant was issued, and asked to speak to the individual in charge of their fugitive task force. A lady on the other end of the phone line politely informed the agent that everyone was out until Monday. Knowing the Municipal Ontario Police Force had little interest in the case, the agent decided to wait and bide his time over the weekend.

With Missouri wanted posters passed throughout the trailer park and on the doors of both the daughter's and mom's trailers, the agent was counting on the cons being conned. The agent's hope rested on the poster's vehicle description and his own Missouri plates. When the mom and daughter saw the wanted posters, they would begin to understand why someone appeared to be watching them— the Missouri insurance investigator was looking for a Missouri fugitive driving around in a vehicle just like theirs! What a coincidence! They would then relax and lower their guard. At least that was the hope.

The agent's next step was to stay away, allow the fugitive family to review the posters, verify there was a fugitive from Missouri, and that the wanted poster's phone number was a Missouri number. Connecting all the dots laid out for them would lead them to a picture the agent had painted, and they would relax.

On Saturday, the fugitive recovery agent prepared a complete report of his investigation, each family member's profile, and their accompanying list of crimes and warrants. Knowing Ontario P.D. was little help, the agent planned on visiting the County Sheriff on Monday morning. The reports on the County Sheriff's Office the agent had read, emailed to him by his researcher, led him to believe the Malheur County Sheriff's Office officers were no-nonsense law enforcement officers who *would* act.

Another concern that had begun to take on more importance than capturing the fugitive was the danger the agent believed the seven-year-old girl faced. This family had a drug and crime problem. Every day this little girl was with them, she was in danger. The recovery agent believed her safety needed to be of paramount importance during the operation.

The fugitive recovery agent called a Federal Marshal, with whom he had prior contact, and began relaying to her information regarding the fugitives. If the local police were not going to act, the agent hoped the federal authorities would. It was clear several violated federal statutes might allow the Feds to intervene if necessary.

An independent agent in the field's biggest problem is the disinterest that law enforcement often shows towards a private individuals' active investigation. Too often, the authorities do not care because it is not their investigation. The agent acting as a private insurance investigator or fugitive recovery agent specializing in bail bond fraud, and tracking, arresting, and returning fugitives who are on the run must often operate alone.

Acting in a private capacity itself can draw the scorn of the authorities. However, the Marshal this agent contacted was a professional who cared more about capturing a fugitive and the safety of a little girl. That is why most fugitive recovery agents hold the Federal Marshals in high regard. The Federal Marshals are the cream of the crop when tracking, finding, and arresting fugitives. They are professional, and they care. They risk their lives each day to take one more fugitive off the streets, protect the innocent, and prevent new victims. And that is the worthy cause of tracking and apprehending criminals: preventing new victims by stopping another crime before it occurs.

During an arrest in Massachusetts, a fugitive recovery agent had once been told by a responding officer, who answered the call, '*You know we hate coming to these calls.*' The officer referred to the **calls** a police station receives when a private party such as a bail-bonding agent or a fugitive recovery agent attempts an arrest. When, during the arrest, a commotion occurs and the police are forced to respond, they are not happy.

This fugitive recovery agent operating in Massachusetts had arrested a large female, who had a warrant out of Colorado for domestic violence. After her cuffing, she screamed bloody murder. It was all the fugitive recovery agent could do to remain calm, hold on, and maintain some control until the police arrived.

After receiving the statement of displeasure from the police officer, who had to respond to the call, the agent wondered, '*Would you rather come to a call after my fugitive beats up someone else and leaves them in a bloody heap on the floor of your city? Would that be a better call?*'

Would a better call be a Colorado fugitive that severely injures a Massachusetts citizen in a blind rage, who ran their streets because no one wanted to come out, arrest and return him or her to Colorado? Would that be a better call?

Or what about an individual with three D.U.I.'s who flees Colorado and runs to Massachusetts to avoid going to jail? Is a better call the accident he or she causes that kills an innocent family of four? Would an accident caused by a fugitive drunk driver from Colorado, where a family is mangled in a massive steel coffin because no one from Colorado came after the fugitive, be a better call?'

What do you think? What is the better call?

And this is the endgame of tracking fugitives who jump bond, who refuse to appear in court after their release from jail. Every time a runner is captured, a citizen who may have become the fugitive's next victim is not victimized. Each time a fugitive recovery agent arrests a criminal, they have tracked down; they terminate the possibility of a new crime being committed. Like the movie **Minority Report**, bail-bonding agents stop a potential crime before it occurs. And the fantastic truth held in the fact of this action is that *no one will ever notice*. A fugitive on the run is dangerous simply because they have decided the laws and the court system designed to protect innocent citizens do not apply to them.

There are no statistics for crimes that will not be committed or victims who will now not exist because of the capture and removal from the streets of one fugitive. However, there will also be no moments of suffering, grief, or loss. One criminal in custody has the potential to save at least one innocent citizen from the victimization that was waiting for them in the shadows where that fugitive lurked. *Many times, a bail-bonding agent or fugitive recovery agent is a victim's last hope for Justice.*

In Oregon, the fugitive recovery agent believed that his best hope to save a little girl and prevent at least one new crime was to get a fugitive off the street. The Federal Marshal he contacted agreed. As he reported his progress, the Marshal forwarded the recovery agent's information to the F.B.I. Office in Oregon.

During the waiting weekend, the recovery agent tried to stay away from the operational area, allowing the situation to cool down.

On Monday morning, the fugitive recovery agent drove to the County Sheriff's Department with his investigative packet, complete with fugitive pictures, warrants, and intel. The fugitive recovery agent had also narrowed the search for the mother's worksite to one hotel in Ontario. Because of the flight risk and the potential for violence, it would be unwise for the agent himself to attempt to arrest his target, save the little girl across town, then ride off into the sunset. The two locations needed simultaneous attention.

The agent's new plan was to attempt to coordinate with the Sheriff's Department and Oregon D.H.S. so that all could be accomplished quickly and without complications.

At the Malheur County Sheriff's Office, the officer and the recovery agent met. The officer listened intently as the agent explained the dangers, risk of flight, and potential harm facing the seven-year-old girl.

After leaving the county sheriff's office, the fugitive recovery agent contacted the Florida Sheriff's Office, where the original warrant for the mom remained active. The officer in charge of extraditions was now available, and the recovery agent requested that the officer personally call the Malheur County Sheriff's Office to put the heat on.

The fugitive recovery agent faxed the Florida officials a map pinpointing the trailers' exact location where the fugitive family was living. He also included new information on the mom's employment. The idea was to hit the Malheur County Sheriff's Department from two different directions: an investigator on the ground and the Sheriff's Department in Florida. The Florida Sheriff's Department would have more legal standing in the Malheur County Sheriff's Department's eyes than one lone fugitive recovery agent.

The Florida officer assured the agent they would call the Malheur Sheriff's Office immediately following their conversation. He did.

Within three hours, the mother was in custody, and a standoff was taking place at the trailer where the little girl was living. The grandmother's arrest at work had gone smoothly, but the sheriff's officers were now at the primary residence, and the granddad was refusing to open the door.

A sheriff's deputy contacted the fugitive recovery agent with the news. The agent suggested the officer inform the granddad that if he did not open the door, the F.B.I. and Federal Marshals would become involved. The agent made the officer aware of his communication with the Federal Marshals and suggested that grandad could face several federal charges for transporting the child across state lines if the Defendant would not open the door. Because the little girl had been under the supervision of Colorado D.H.S., her removal from that State had been illegal.

After the information was relayed to the granddad, he opened the door, allowing the Sheriff's Deputies and Oregon D.H.S. to check on and evaluate the grandchild's safety and well-being. Oregon D.H.S. then initiated a case file for her continued protection while the family was in Oregon. A sheriff's deputy also informed the granddad that if he attempted to take the little girl out of their State and away from Oregon D.H.S.'s oversight, kidnapping charges would follow.

At this point, although the recovery agent was prepared to take the fugitive back to Colorado, the sheriff in the Colorado county from which she'd fled refused to enter an extraditable warrant into the National Crime Data network for this purpose. The sheriff's response was in direct contrast to the wanted posters *hanging on the walls of his own jail's lobby*, declaring both the grandma and granddad as 2 of that County's 10 Most Wanted.

Posters of the County's 10 Most Wanted decorate that Colorado County Jail's reception area walls, greeting visitors when they enter. At the time of this investigation, both the criminal female maître d' and her husband's wanted posters accompanied the other eight hanging pictures. However, when notified that both were available for extradition, the sheriff was not interested. So much for the most wanted, who are not always really wanted.

The disinterest by some in law enforcement to have wanted criminals returned from out of State is another critical problem that encourages fugitives to run. No one wants them back. If they are stealing, cheating, and victimizing citizens in other jurisdictions, it may not matter to those who issued the warrant. It is a dangerous attitude that leads to the unspoken game of Musical States. *'Please do not return my criminals, and I won't return yours!'*

When a bail bondsman, either in person or through an agent he or she contracts with, arrests a fugitive, the costs of that fugitive's return is borne by the bail bonding agent, not the State, or the county, or the sheriff's department in the county from which they ran. The bonding agent must pay all costs. And though various sheriffs and district attorney departments do not want these fugitives returned, we are fortunate that this attitude is not yet mainstream in Colorado.

The fugitive recovery agent prepared for the fugitive's first court appearance the day following the fugitive's arrest. After her arrest, the culprit was held overnight in the Malheur County Jail and would appear in court the next morning. The fugitive recovery agent did not want her out on a pre-trial bond. If that happened, he knew he would never see her again. The Colorado agent took a new investigative packet that included his fugitive's background, warrant history, fugitive status from two states, and the details of each of the Defendant's family members she lived with to the courthouse. He then handed them over to the district attorney.

Because of the agent's efforts, this fugitive did not receive a low-cost, *Crime-for-Free* Bond and was extradited to Florida to

face Justice. Upon her arrival in Florida, she received an eight-year prison sentence.

This mother of crime had been the leader of the pack. Even her work at the motel placed others in danger of being victimized. It is not hard to clean a motel room while keeping an eye out for any I.D.'s, money, or forgotten jewelry left by those on vacation. While the innocent visitors are out enjoying the sites, the fraudster maid is on the prowl. This lady's criminal profile was professional fraud, and she had obtained work at the perfect place to further her criminal career at another's expense.

After this fugitive's capture, the story took a sad turn; Oregon D.H.S. decided to leave the little girl in the care and custody of the fugitive granddad. The same man who had two warrants out of Colorado for drugs and probation violation would now be allowed to care for the well-being of this young girl. Why? Because he received his freedom through Colorado's Pretrial **Crime-for- Free** program, and no one wanted him back.

Oregon could not prosecute him for the crimes he committed in Colorado, and so, he was free.

Neither his son nor daughter feared their forced return either, as both had been granted their own **Crime-for-Free** bonds. No one was coming after them. They were freed by the State in which they were initially arrested, not by a commercial bondsman. They ran from the jurisdictions that did not care that they were now in Oregon, free to prey on others. Colorado Pretrial was not accountable for the two fugitives whose release they had secured. Oregon may have cared, but they had no jurisdiction over charges originating from Colorado and Florida.

Oregon authorities will now have to wait until one of these family members commits a new crime in their State. They will have to wait until there is another victim. Our prayer is that the next victim will not be the seven-year-old girl.

The main fugitive was taken off the streets and will not create another victim in Oregon, not for eight years. The fugitive recovery agent who handled the case prevented a potential new crime before it ever happened. That is the difference between commercial bail and a state's Pretrial program.

Bail-bonding agents will go after a fugitive who crosses the state line. We will track them, stop them, arrest them, then return them to face justice. We are accountable.

A state's Pretrial program does not include the recapture of a fugitive—a criminal suspect they've freed—who goes on the run. They will only release them. They are not accountable to return them.

It is interesting to note that Oregon does not have commercial bail. They feel it does not serve the public interest. They do have a large **Catch and Release** program that allows for the release of their defendants after they pay a fee to the court for their bond. They also hang out a welcome mat to fugitives from other states who have warrants but do not want to be taken back to face the consequences of their previous crimes.

A television documentary on the tactics of fugitives fleeing Washington State to find refuge in Oregon was very telling. During the showing, the program reported that Oregon currently had a 40% Failure to Appear record. Four out of ten people arrested for any crime in Oregon decide they do not need to appear in court. After they make their freedom payment, with assistance from the State, at taxpayer expense, they are free to go. **'See ya. Bye!'** When they fail to appear back in court, their victims are left stranded in the justice system's no-man's land, and a new innocent awaits victimization.

Ironically, Oregon decided it was better suited to play bail bondsman than the bail-bonding agents it banned, the State itself claiming the 10% fee for each criminal suspect they release. And although critics of bail like to condemn commercial bail as greedy—keeping poor people in jail because they can't afford to pay the premium of a bail bond—Oregon is not held to the same standards. It appears it is okay for a state to demand the 10% fee to free those who can afford to pay the cost while keeping their poor people in jail. A 10% payoff to the state coffers and **Crime-for-Free BAIL** is borne.

Chapter 1

And now, as we see rioters filled with hate, burning, looting, threatening others, attacking those who disagree, we know the result of bail reform. These riots have nothing to do with the death of George Floyd. These rioters care nothing about Mr. Floyd or his family. They are free to destroy, steal, loot, and burn due to the freedom and encouragement they have received from those who hold power in Oregon and many media outlets. It began with bail reform, allowing individuals to turn Justice into a revolving door where the criminals are the new victims. And the real victims? They are simply an inconvenience. And as the barriers that prevented violent hearts from erupting to destroy, burn, threaten, and murder others are taken down, we will see an increase in violence and destruction. Seattle, Portland, Chicago, and New York are all cities that have chosen to honor criminals with unchecked freedom, encouraging anyone with a desire to steal, cheat, burn or loot to roam the streets at will while restricting the freedoms of honest and law-abiding citizens.

And across America, as governments provide taxpayer-funded **Crime-for-Free** programs, fugitives are stealing, robbing, and *criming* their way from State to State, without any fear they will be arrested or be required to answer for their crimes. They leave in their wake the wreckage and ruined lives of those they have victimized while they rob, drink, or beat their way through life, at another's expense. The bail reform movement crossing America reforms nothing. It is merely the American victim's sell-out and the first step in the justice system's breakdown. Blindly releasing all criminals and defunding the police is their end-game—destruction and anarchy.

Caring about the victim of a crime always makes for great T.V. Sheriffs and politicians alike want to be on camera, condemning the crime against persons, claiming they will not stop until they catch the perpetrator! However, once the accused goes on the run and the T.V. cameras are turned off, the victim is left alone. No one cares anymore. No one wants to hear about what the victim suffered or lost. The case disappears with the fugitive crossing the state line, running off into the sunset.

Four fugitives fled to Oregon with one innocent little girl who was forced to go on the run with them. In Ontario, Oregon, they were momentarily stopped in their tracks by a fugitive recovery agent's investigation. One fugitive was arrested and returned to Florida to face Justice. The other three remained free. Why? The captured runner obtained her release with a commercial bond. The other three gained freedom through their State's *Crime-for-Free* Programs. The little girl? She is currently in the care of these fugitives. *Sometimes...crime does seem to pay.*

Chapter 2: Kidnapped - The Justice System
A True Story

The parents were frightened. A north-side gang had kidnaped their son for failing to pay a drug debt. If the parents did not pay the debt, their son would be killed. That was the call I received one day as a new bail-bonding agent in Denver, Colorado.

Having posted this man's bond, I was now considered by law as his jailor. He was in my custody.

The term "in my custody" does not mean a defendant is handcuffed to my feet. It means I have the jurisdiction to enforce rules I wish to set and arrest my Defendant at any time, day, or night. The Power to Arrest is the power to protect the financial risk a bondsman takes when he or she posts a bond. It is a civil agreement the Defendant enters with his bail agent when he signs the bond.

When a defendant makes bail, the Defendant has not attained freedom. In Colorado, their release on bail is considered a continuation of their incarceration. Their transfer on bail is from the jail they were held in to the bail bonding agent's jail. However, the bail agent's jail is not a building, with bars and a cot in a corner. A bail agent's jail usually is anywhere in the city or the State of Colorado that the Defendant may wish to go.

If a defendant fails to go to court or a bail agent believes a defendant is packing their bags for an extended vacation, the bail agent plays a travel agent's role, rearranging the Defendant's itinerary. Bail agents and fugitive recovery agents (people hired to arrest fugitives) can receive a nasty reputation when a poorly planned arrest makes the news. Yet, in America, hundreds of arrests are made weekly, safely, and quietly, by fugitive recovery agents. It is a dangerous profession, but one in which many honorable men and women work, without pay, unless they capture the fugitive they chase.

After being hired as a bail bond agent, I was given a pair of handcuffs and told I could arrest my own fugitives. But in this case, my Defendant was not trying to flee. He was being held for ransom.

The office manager of the bail company I worked for did not want to get involved. These were the days of extreme gang violence in Denver, and the manager did not harbor a death wish. Calling the police wasn't an option: The Defendant was in my custody and was my responsibility.

The decision to save the boy's life was in my court, and following the scriptural insight to 'pray without ceasing,' I did and headed to the address provided by the Defendant's parents.

The location was an older apartment house off Colfax Ave., Denver's main east-west drag. Once there, constant in prayer, I entered the building, climbed the stairs, and tramped down the hall. I knocked, using the old, friendly knock technique, claiming I was a friend. I was not.

A gangbanger opened the door. I could see my Defendant sitting on the couch in his underwear, on the far side of the room. Ignoring everyone else in the room, I said, *"Hey man, the court called and said you didn't show up today."* Even though there was no such hearing, it seemed like a good thing to say at the time.

"*What court,*" the Defendant asked.

"*Arapahoe,*" I answered, feigning annoyance. *"I didn't have you set for court, but I'm just telling you what they said when they called me this morning. Either you come with me now, and we get this straightened out, or I'll call the police, and they can straighten it out."* I used my strict; I'm the Bondsman approach.

One of my problems has always been that I cannot debate with people. I am not a debater.

It was a ridiculous conversation: me standing at the door and my Defendant in his underwear on a couch across the room, as three babysitting, hostage-takers silently hovered about, listening. With a veiled threat of police involvement, I was hoping no one would ask, *"Hey, how'd you know he was here? Who gave you this address?"* No one did.

Finally, I turned directly to the man holding the door ajar and spoke to him. *"This is crazy. My records don't show any hearing today, but unless he appears in court this morning, the court claims it will order the bond forfeited. I'm not going to risk losing my money."*

"You a bondsman?" asked the Guardian of the Door.

"Yea," I replied, producing a business card. *"If you ever get in a jam, call me. I never let my friends sit in jail,"* I assured him.

My Defendant was given his pants and was putting them on when I said, *"I'll bring you right back after this is over. But hurry up, let's go! I've got other things to do."* Another area I continually struggle with is patience.

Pants pulled up, my Defendant walked out of the room, and we eased down the hall shadowed by two of the Kidnappers in Training.

"This is a pain," I stated out loud for the benefit of the nearest Shadow. *"I've got too much to do today, and this screws up everything."* He backed off, letting us walk out of the building, but trailed us a half a block to where my parked car waited.

Once out of the building, my Defendant breathed a sigh of relief. *"Thank God,"* he whispered.

"You better thank God," I hissed back.

Him saying, 'Thank God," as casually as if he were saying, 'Boy, I'm glad that's all over,' disturbed me. He was not saying, *'Thank you, God, for saving me.'* He was saying, *'Thank God, I'm out of that mess.'* His fate as a metro crime statistic, a lifeless body dumped in an alley, had been thwarted, but the mention of God had been only a secondary, passing statement.

During this summer stretch, gang killings in Denver seemed to be part of a daily menu. It was not really a big deal, except for the police ... and those who were being killed, of course. However, to this man, who had moments earlier sat in the care and company of those who were planning his execution, God was no more than a brief word in a sigh of relief.

On that day, we walked by the grace of God, not because I was cunning or daring. I had walked in fear, hiding under the hope that the Lord would be with me. Somehow, the right words had come to me, and they allowed the confusion of the surprise visit to baffle those who had dark plans for my clients' son. The hostage-takers did not know what to do.

The Spirit of the Lord descended upon that room, and an air of peace settled amidst the danger of the moment. The atmosphere of peace kept us safe. The confusion kept them off balance, and we had walked away.

After we left, I immediately drove the man to the Arapahoe District Court, where his present criminal case was pending, and surrendered him in open court. It appeared to me that he would be safer locked up than running the streets, trying to dodge those who wanted him dead. His life had meant nothing to that gang, except for the money they'd hoped to collect from his parents for not killing him.

Some people *should* spend a few days in jail.

Critics of bail-bonding claim that across America, hundreds and thousands of innocent people languish in jail because they are poor. The rich can make bail while the poor sit behind bars. Incredibly, critics enjoy dividing everything between two variables. There are rich, and there are poor. That's all. People in between do not exist. These critics then claim that cash bail is unfair and unconstitutional. They base their argument on the premise of 'innocent until proven guilty." According to that logic, nobody committed a crime; therefore, no one should be held in jail pending their court case. They would have us believe that police, having nothing better to do, no real criminals to pursue, spend their days and nights arresting the underprivileged because they have no money. Police officers cruise the neighborhoods they serve, seeking out innocent poor people to put in jail.

At first, critics of cash bail claimed that only individuals arrested for violent crimes, or those who may be a threat to society, should be held without bail. However, this contradicts the very premise on which they lean. It is also not an honest evaluation of their final intention. The end game of bail reform is the overall destruction and ruin of the justice system and the freeing of all jailed criminal suspects.

Currently, in many states, an individual is arrested and jailed because a police officer has probable cause to believe they have committed a crime or have an outstanding warrant for their arrest. Once locked up, the arrestee will typically have a bond set. The monetary amount of the initial bond is determined by a bond schedule pre-set by a court. The original bond amount is a preliminary guideline the jail will follow before the criminal suspect ever makes his or her first appearance in court. The bond is a point of release with control and accountability.

Bail Reform promotes a theme claiming thousands of jailed innocents are incarcerated because they have no money. New York agreed and instituted bail reform that mandated the release without bail of everyone arrested for a non-violent crime. Since their new system of freedom, crime in New York has soared. Bank Robbers, burglars, and thieves have all been celebrating in the streets and on camera. One bank robber facing multiple bank robbery charges thanked Democrats as he walked out of jail. In front of the cameras, he thanked those who secured his freedom without bail. He later was rearrested after robbing yet another bank.

A criminal group from South America, hearing of New York's immediate release policy for non-violent offenders, promptly left for New York. This group then ran a burglary ring in the heart of New York, knowing if caught, they would immediately be freed and could return home. And eventually, they were caught, quickly released from jail, and able to return to South America without penalties or facing Justice. Bail reform at its finest is little more than a draw for criminals who know they can operate without fear of repercussions.

To think individuals intent on a criminal lifestyle do not calculate risk factors before plying their trade is judicial blindness at its peak. And the key to their calculation is the probability of jail—no jail, no trial, and freedom once more.

Bail reform advocates hide their real intention in the false sound bite that thousands of individuals are jailed across America because they are poor. They then promoted the release of all non-violent offenders without bail. Others support a computer printout from the Arnold Foundation that claims purity in calculating an offender's risk to re-offend and their threat to society. Of course, those murdered or victimized by the release of criminal suspects through the computerized, scientific algorithm from the Arnold Foundation might beg to differ… if they still could.

The first move of bail reform was to push for the release of non-violent offenders. Their next goal, the freedom of anyone jailed, is now becoming public. Non-profits loaded with cash for the sole purpose of bonding out criminal suspects are sprouting up. According to a Fox News report, dated August 9, 2020, one Minnesota non-profit has enjoyed a flood of donations, and flush with cash, is posting the bonds of anyone arrested. These bonds include freeing people charged with serious crimes, including sexual assault, attempted murder, and murder.

As stated in the Fox News article, the Minnesota non-profit with a 35 million slush fund to post bonds for anyone arrested enjoys the monetary support of many political contributors, including but not limited to several Biden campaign staffers. This dangerous escalation in the freeing of criminal suspects without regard to public safety, without accountability, should put fear in the heart of every American.

While a Minnesota non-profit is flush in cash, freeing anyone arrested, New York will not require this group to liberate its own jailed criminal suspects. Promoted as a form of justice reform, New York instituted bail reform that first freed non-violent defendants but has grown in compassion to now release their violent offenders without bail.

As reported in a New York Post article in May of 2020, '*A Brooklyn man accused of attacking a woman so viciously that he left her in a vegetative state had been charged in two prior assaults this year – but was twice freed without bail, the Post has learned.*'

Another criminal suspect was accused of attacking the top N.Y.P.D. Chief was freed without bail after his arrest for the attack. What an encouragement this release should give other street thugs who would rather fight a police officer when confronted while committing a crime than to go quietly. If they are hurt while fighting off a police officer during an arrest, they can claim police brutality.

And throughout New York, crime has skyrocketed. Non-violent and violent crime together, hand in hand. One congressional rep claimed that crime has skyrocketed because people cannot afford to buy a loaf of bread. That is amazing. And now that we understand the reason for rapists, attackers, bank robbers, drug dealers, thieves, and those on the road committing drive-by shootings, we should establish a free bread bakery. Everyone would get a free loaf of bread, and crime would be no more.

The new bail reform could include a free loaf of bread for each prisoner released.

The truth about crime raging, and out of control criminals began not with the George Floyd murder, but with the bail reform system pushed off as Justice re-visited. The bail reform incorporated within cities from Seattle and Chicago to New York laid the groundwork for the destruction, violence, and surging crime rates we see today.

Even the riots, looting, violence, and murder in these same cities were born in the seeds of bail reform. Granting criminals' power without restrictions or accountability, allowing individuals the right to riot, threaten others, stab, shoot, burn and loot, are all part of the bail reform push. Reform bail, free all criminal suspects, defund the police.

These violent, hateful individuals ripping apart the fabric of society care nothing about George Floyd or Black lives, including the black lives they have taken during their riots. These rioters of Justice have murdered numerous black men. Other black men and women have had their businesses looted and burned in the name of Justice by these same rioters. Black men and women who worked hard to make a living and care for their families saw it all go up in smoke by individuals not satisfied with stealing everything from their stores but who had to burn them out as well.

The rioters' hatred and madness were released and freed because others decided their crimes should not be punished but rewarded. They are encouraged by politicians, many in the media, and sideline cheerleaders. They claim they are anti-fascists. However, they only need to glimpse in a mirror to see the hateful fascists they seek. They are criminals, let free to riot, threaten, and murder. They are corrupted actors, taking advantage of soundbites to justify their violent evil hatred and corruption.

From non-violence to violence, bail reform has borne the child of its inception. These cities where violent rioters and criminals are emerging first began with the birth of bail reform.

Bond Schedules

How a bond is first set in the states that still care about their citizenry is often via a bond schedule. A standard bond schedule follows several factors, beginning with the charge for which the criminal suspect was arrested. When the seriousness of the offense is low, the bail is lower. Other criteria that come into play are an individual's criminal arrest history, previous convictions, and a record of court appearances or lack thereof. The Defendant's estimated risk of danger to society or a victim once they bond out of jail is also considered.

After weighing all the mitigating factors, the setting of the bond takes place. This bond amount, however, is only temporary. It is a pre-set monetary amount that will allow the criminal suspect immediate freedom. If the arrestee does not post a bond for any reason, they will generally appear in court before a magistrate or judge within twenty-four hours to review their charges. They will be allowed an opportunity to address the issue of a bond at these hearings.

Furthermore, although critics of bail like to maintain that everyone held in jail is innocent, the premise of innocence until proven guilty is a legal stance, not a fact. Until the resolution of each court case, one cannot throw out reality on a premise. The average conviction rate of individuals arrested and charged with a crime or violation of the law is 80% and 90%.

That fact alone suggests that 80% to 90% of those held in jails are guilty. They are not all innocent.

Critics also claim that those sitting in jail have a higher conviction rate than those released on bail. They suggest individuals incarcerated plea cases just because they are locked up. In truth, there are many reasons those held in jail until trial have more convictions than those on bond. Bond critics ignore those reasons and use math magic when presenting conviction percentages of incarcerated inmates versus Defendants' conviction rates out of jail on bond. These conviction percentages can then be used as math magic to astound their followers.

A few reform advocates claim that the conviction rate for those confined in jail is 11% higher than those released on bail. The figures quoted are not qualified but simplified. If they are in jail, they are more likely to be convicted because…they are incarcerated.

Since between 85% to 90% of the individuals I post a bond for either plead guilty or are found guilty in a trial before a court, I have no idea where others get their 11% higher conviction rate. The people I bond out of jail have their freedom until the resolution of their case, yet their conviction rate is still somewhere in the 90 percentiles.

And why do some people sit in jail until the resolution of their case while others do not? Although there are always exceptions, the basics are easy to understand and seldom have anything to do with the wealth a person may or may not have.

Burned Bridges

Families and friends of individuals with long records of arrests and criminal convictions can tire of trying to help their loved ones. They grow weary of empty promises, paying out money only to have the criminal suspect return to his or her criminal life after their release from jail.

In jail, these repeat offenders plead and beg their family and friends to help them post a bond. They promise everything, but once released, follow through with nothing. Their gratitude for others' kindness is short-lived. Many times, they will turn on those who helped with their release from jail. When a friend or family member asks why they are not keeping their promises to change, the criminal suspect becomes resentful and argumentative. '*Stay out of my life*,' is a common refrain.

While in jail, many cry tears to squeeze out sympathy from the listener on the other end of the phone. Once they are no longer behind bars, they care for only one person: themselves. But now, rather than help the individual get out of jail on bail once more, the friend or family member finally feels it is time for their loved one to sit and review their life. And so, the criminal suspect, having burned all his bridges, sits.

A Lesson Learned is a Lesson Earned

I have received calls from family members and friends of incarcerated individuals who ask that the Defendant remains in jail.

Whether drugs or drinking and driving, the Defendant's family member, mom, or dad, sister, or brother, pleads that I leave their loved one in jail in hopes their loved one can realize how they are destroying their life.

On the outside, their loved one has refused to listen to their families warning or advice. However, once arrested and in jail, the reality of their actions and the consequences can have a sobering effect. Their incarceration then becomes a form of shock treatment, teaching the truth of life.

There are times when leaving a person in jail is a better kindness than immediately releasing them. Even as I write this, I just hung up with a father whose son was arrested. He stated he wanted his son to stay in jail long enough to sober up, not from drinking but from drugs. While he was free, the son would not change. Even when forced into a drug rehabilitation center, his stay lasted no more than a day. After checking in, he would take himself out before the end of the second day.

An arrest and an immediate release can sometimes have little life-changing impact. But an arrest where the individual sits in jail a few days before being released can open their eyes, becoming a significant force for altering their behavior.

Danger

Crimes of violence that pose a danger to society can increase a bond amount, thereby depriving the criminal suspect of their freedom between court dates. Others have anger issues that rise to violence that threatens others.

Unstable individuals with mental issues who have no control over their actions and hurt others should not be allowed to run free. In a few cities where courts or city leaders have determined that these mentally unstable individuals should not be jailed or locked up, the citizen on the street becomes the next crime statistic. These are the people, innocent citizens—victims—who are never talked about when mentioning bail reform.

That a criminal and violent predator should be freed after beating, threatening, stabbing, or otherwise terrorizing a community simply because it is claimed he or she has a mental illness defies logic. What criminal suspect does not have some aspect of a mental illness that drives them to cheat, steal, injure, threaten, or hurt others? Yet, Seattle's compassion for the criminals labeled mentally ill continually surpasses peaceful citizens' rights daily.

In Oregon, during the height of their fire season in 2020, with record-breaking flames burning forests, homes, with at least 35 dead, an arson suspect who confessed to setting fires was released within hours of his arrest. He was released on his signature, and no bail was required because he was homeless. Within 12 hours of his first arrest and release, he was arrested again. His crime? Once again, this unfortunate individual was out setting fires. Was his first release was no more than the compassion of insanity. And this is bail reform. Meanwhile, the fires rage on.

Career Criminals

Career criminals have only one never-ending agenda: to cheat, rob, and steal their way through life. Once they find themselves in jail, they have no intention of changing anything but their current surroundings. The design of their entire life plan is at the expense of others. They may not be physically violent, but they are dangerous, nonetheless. Their danger is evident in their attitude: that others should pay for their lifestyle, which often includes drugs, drinking, or cheating others.

One should also note that violent criminal suspects, at one time, were also non-violent. The separation between non-violent and violent is but one act, one moment when one crosses the line, either intentionally or by accident. A shoplifter who pushes away a store security agent, who then falls and hits their head, suffering injury, has crossed the line. Non-violent criminal suspects of today *are* the potential violent criminals of tomorrow.

As for career criminals, these are the individuals who are usually the pros of getting out of jail, using Pretrial as their preferred choice for freedom. They are always innocent, and it is everyone else's fault.

A problem only arises for them when their excuses and cons no longer work. Then they must sit in jail and wait until the resolution of their case before they can hit the streets again.

In Louisiana, bail reform has hit a new low. According to an investigative series by W.W.L.T.V.'s Mike Perlstein on 10/26/2018, a New Orleans Mayor boasted of the city's crime-fighting on the local front-page newspaper while freeing the criminal suspects, before the article could even be printed. After New Orleans Mayor, Latoya Cantrell, bragged about a police operation that netted dozens of drug traffickers' arrest, it was revealed that the Mayor's top assistant was using a cash fund to bail out as many as seven of these traffickers at the same time.

While the Mayor publicly bragged that, '**We are not going to let up until we ensure that they are off the streets,**' his aid, Joshua Cox, the Mayor's director of strategic planning, was releasing seven of those street dealers back onto the streets, according to the article. The releases were secured using a special cash fund Cox created called the **Freedom Fund**. Supported by donors and activists, this method of freeing selected arrested individuals assured some that they would not need to fear arrest. The Mayor and the Mayor's assistant would have their back.

In one case, an ex-felon with five felony convictions, including assault with a dangerous weapon, was bailed out twice by this group organized by the Mayor's assistant.

Another convicted felon had his bond posted by the Freedom Fund after he had served a two-year prison sentence for assault in Texas, only to be arrested again in New Orleans. And that is the underlying purpose and end-result of bail reform. Free criminal suspects without accountability or regard to the victims they have attacked, robbed, cheated, and hurt.

This Freedom Fund, overseen by Joshua Cox, which was used like a Criminal Get Out of Jail Free card for the benefit of those arrested, boasted a high percentage of released defendants, reappearing in court. The promoters of the Freedom Fund claim that 92% of the individuals they bond out appear in court. This number, however, is offered without any proof. Their records are not open to the public. Furthermore, they do not state whether 92% refers to a defendant's first court date or every court appearance after that. The big game of failing to show for court often allows defendants one or two appearances, giving them time to assess the situation and the risks they face. After the risks are known, they can then determine whether to return for their court date. The truth of appearing in court is that everyone goes to court … until they choose not to.

Habitual Failures to Appear

In one case, after posting a bond and while driving the Defendant to his vehicle, the bail agent listened to the Defendant brag about his previous cases. He'd had one in California and another in Iowa. The freed inmate shared how he bailed out of Iowa and crossed the state line to avoid answering the charges that caused his arrest.

In California, he had a different game plan. After being released from jail following his first arrest, he refused to appear in court. His intentional failure to show for court, subsequent arrest, and re-bonding out of jail happened several times. He would get arrested, bail out of jail, and never go to court. Eventually, the court, tiring of his case, dropped the charges against him. Who needs a lawyer when repeated failures to appear can cause a case dismissal? These are all the lessons learned by those charged with violations of any law. Don't show and don't go unless the going is far away.

When this bail-bonding agent delivered the Defendant to his car, the replay of the Defendant's words haunted the agent's thoughts. The next morning, the bail agent contacted the Defendant and asked if they could meet. The Defendant, thinking all was good, agreed and met the bail agent. At their meeting, the agent slapped on a pair of cuffs.

"Hey, what's going on? I haven't missed court yet," cried the Defendant.

"I know," replied the agent. "And I intend that you won't miss court. I am refunding your money and putting you back in jail. You can sit in jail until your case is over."

"Why?" complained the Defendant.

"Because it is about time you faced a court for the charges filed against you."

Although there is always a chance a person can accidentally miss their court date, many criminal suspects choose not to go to court, and that number continues to rise. Each time these defendants are arrested and make bail, they promise to appear. However, their actions prove they have no intention of appearing. They simply go on the run until they are caught once more and returned to jail. Then the process begins again.

These individuals have no respect for the law, for those they hurt, or even for their promises, which they dish out like leftovers. They will say anything, promise more, and plead with tears and sadness, but their underlying will is that they will not appear in court once they are released.

At some point, these criminal suspects will end up sitting in jail with no one willing to step forward and help them. Also, a court seeing their flagrant disregard for the justice system and the laws that everyone else follows will set a higher bond, knowing these individuals will run once released.

The fact is that the reasons why some criminal suspects remain in jail until the conclusion of their case can vary, but seldom is it only because they are poor. There are often many reasons in their lives and past that create red flags. These warning signs tell the court of this individual's probability of committing more crimes or failing to appear in court. Family and friends see the red flags and refuse to step up to help. Even bail-bonding agents who know the danger signs and see flags waving in the wind will refuse to post their bond.

Vagabonds

Although these are individuals with little or no money, they remain in jail not because they are poor but because they have a history of no shows. They do not show up to work because, by choice, they have no job. They live from place to place, wherever they can mooch a bed and a free meal. These are those who have chosen a lifestyle requiring others to pay for their existence continually.

These are not individuals who have lost their jobs due to unforeseen circumstances or others who have fallen on hard times. These criminal suspects are professional parasites that, if freed, will vanish once again. They will never appear in court unless forced to do so.

Until proven guilty, the premise of innocence is a right afforded everyone in a court of law for their protection. However, the reality that the criminal suspect may be responsible must also be considered. Otherwise, why arrest anyone? If everyone is genuinely innocent, then there is no reason for anyone's arrest. We can disband the police force in each community and close the jails because there are no criminals. Alternatively, perhaps we should round up and jail all the phony victims who claim a crime has been committed against them. Jail them for making false police reports. Since there are no guilty, there can be no victims.

In my operation, my dealings are not with the rich. My transactions are with everyday people. I may have only two to three cases a year where an individual lacks the finances to make bail or pay a premium fee. Most of my refusals to post an individual's bond have to do with a person's criminal past, deceit, and risk factors having nothing to do with a lack of money.

Ninety-nine percent of the people who contact me wanting a bond posted have the premium fee ready and can pay it before I even request it. However, my concern is not first and foremost, with the fees charged, but the criminal charges facing the defendant, the honesty of those contacting me, and the risk factors that might determine the defendant's intention to run rather than appear in court. Also, is the defendant a danger to themselves or others? These are the concerns I evaluate before posting a bond.

Across America, more and more individuals realize that freedom from the court and the consequences of their actions are only one state hop away.

The 2015 *USA Today* story on the fugitive next door by Brad Heath points out that these fugitives, after they cross the state line, often continue to break the law. Even some of those initially wanted for minor offenses, once they passed the state line, ended up committing horrible crimes.

Later in 2015, Heath wrote another article about the 350,000 fugitives who roam our country from State to State.

Other articles from papers across the country tell a tale of fugitives running free, unaccounted for, and of no concern to the states that hold the warrants for their arrest. I cannot begin to name them all, but here are a few:

> *Fort Meyers News-Press* (March 2014) Headline: "In Collier, Skirting Extradition May be a State Away"

> *Nashville Tennessean* (March 2014) Headline: "The Short Arm of the Law" (This article refers to how a fugitive need not go far to avoid being returned to jail. One state line suffices.)

> *Green Bay Press-Gazette* (March 2014) Headline: "Fugitives Evade Justice Due to Restricted Warrants." Note: Wisconsin banned bail-bonding and now won't even go after many of their own fugitives who leave the State and head for the safety of the one next door.

At one time, Wisconsin enjoyed the benefits of commercial bail. However, after an investigation revealed a scandal between one bail-bonding company and a judge who wanted enrichment for assuring favorable rulings for the bonding company, bail-bonding was abolished. And this is the absurd overreaction of politicians who desire to punish the entire industry for the acts of one or a few, striking a blow against ordinary intelligence. Why not banish all judges, too, while you're at it? After all, a judge accepted the bribes and had the power to issue the rulings.

Now Wisconsin's fugitives run free, left to victimize new citizens in neighboring states. After Wisconsin instituted and allowed these defendants their freedom through Wisconsin's government-run

Pretrial *Crime-for-Free* programs, the accused are indeed grateful. There will not be any bail agents or fugitive recovery agents on their trail. No one will track them down when they fail to appear in court.

Wisconsin has also become a fugitive-friendly state. Fugitives from other jurisdictions are learning they can avoid prosecution for their crimes if they run to Wisconsin. When criminal suspects are arrested for drunk driving, domestic violence, and various felonies from fraud to theft and other assorted crimes want to escape justice, they seek a safe harbor. These fugitives now know that if they beat it out of their home state and run to Wisconsin, they've found that harbor. I wonder how Wisconsin citizens would feel if they understood that their state aids and abets fugitives? Politicians aid and abet fugitives on the run by making Wisconsin a safe house for those wanted on crimes from other jurisdictions.

Wisconsin also does not allow bail-bonding agents or fugitive recovery agents into their state to arrest and remove these criminals. Their politicians serve a higher calling, leaving their citizens prey for the criminals on the run in America.

It is a state-by-state merry-go-round. The fugitives all riding musical horses, round and round, on the carousel of freedom. Each time the ride stops, the fugitive can hop off, commit a few crimes, and victimize a few innocents until arrested. Afterward, they avoid court by hopping back on the state-sponsored Pretrial carnival ride of freedom.

This process is what I call the "Sellout of the American Victim." These politicians love a picture pose decrying violence and crimes against their citizens. They speak out against domestic violence and drunk drivers and display a lot of TV-determination to bring justice for the victims of these crimes. It is too bad their determination and care for these victims often end at the state line. The laws they enact also throw out a welcome mat to criminals running from warrants in other states. They then turn a blind eye as their own state's criminals cross that magical state boundary and travel down the road to freedom.

Fortunately, in Colorado, the politicians have, thus far, taken the flight of every fugitive to heart. They know that commercial bail agents will pursue these fugitives and ensure justice for their citizens. To date, Colorado legislatures have shown a willingness to let the professionals secure the justice each victim loses when a defendant goes on the run. Colorado legislatures opened the door for commercial bail, and because they did, many victims have been made whole, citizens protected, and many crimes stopped before they happened.

In Colorado, the state legislatures who allowed commercial bail took more than a TV-Smile approach to justice. They knew that bonding agents would strengthen the justice system. These elected officials understand that even when cameras turn off, someone is still out on the streets pursuing fugitives who have hurt, harmed, robbed, and cheated their citizens.

> *The Des Moines Register* (Feb. 10, 2015) Headline: "Fugitives roam free beyond borders."

> *The Greenview News* (March 2014) Headline: "Few Extraditions sought."

Once more, these are only a few of the stories around the country of fugitives running the streets, crossing one state line at a time to avoid prosecution, to avoid justice.

Either a suspect criminal should face justice or should not. Unfortunately, many in the government believe it is okay if suspected criminals do not. They claim the jails are overcrowded; it costs too much to house individuals arrested, who we know are all innocent *until proven guilty*. For these reasons, they feel their Pretrial *Catch and Release* programs are an excellent alternative to jail overcrowding problems and high costs. But at what cost? And why is it that it is the victim who often bears that cost?

Another warning of the dangers and misguided concepts of bail reform's musical cells and crime for free bail bonds comes from a retired Superior Court Judge, former state senator, and San Francisco Board of Supervisors member, Quentin L. Kopp. As Mr. Kopp wrote in an article for the *San Francisco Chronicle* in August 2017:

> The cause du jour for apparently uninformed liberals regarding criminal law is based on a principle that poor defendants

without money are unjustly held in jail pending trial simply because they can't afford bail and are, thus, the objects of unconstitutional discrimination by unequal treatment.

They demand the system be changed, that new 'tools' such as computer algorithms be used to decide whether a defendant can be safely released without depositing bail, and they say that a Pretrial assessment will ensure a released defendant won't endanger the crime victim or other people and will show up for every hearing and trial.

In comparing the new proposed California bail reform law to several other states that had enacted bail reform, the retired Superior Court Judge gave a warning. He shared:

"New Jersey, New Mexico and the District of Columbia have adopted such systems creating a presumption that pretrial "public safety assessment scores" will resolve public safety and court appearance fears of prosecutors, law enforcement officers, and citizens. They call it "reform."

In truth, this sham is one of the most dangerous and misleading legislative efforts I've seen in more than 50 years as a criminal and civil trial lawyer and ten years as a California Superior Court judge.

The former Judge concludes his statement by giving voice to others who are also opposed to California's new bail reform laws. "The alliance of California judges and California District Attorneys associations oppose SB10."

A Democratic New Jersey Assemblyman, Bob Andrzejczak, also voiced his concern. As he stated publicly in a July 3rd letter to the California Assembly Speaker, legislators made a terrible mistake in voting for similar New Jersey legislation last year, calling its implementation **"an absolute disaster."**

The former Judge's conclusion? *'SB10 would be ruinous to California's criminal law system and to California.'*

California citizens can now look to New Jersey, New York, Seattle, Portland, and Chicago to see what is coming. Where bail reform or elimination of bail has freed many, they are rioting in the streets, having the time of their life.

And in the hateful rioting and violence flourishing in the cities where bail reform rules, criminals parade around as warriors of justice, licensed to threaten, stab, shoot, burn and loot. Others now justify their acts for nothing more than political gain.

In Chicago, on August 11th, 2020, a story in Fox News states that a BLM organizer has claimed the looting taking place is reparations. *'That is reparations*,' a BLM organizer said. *'Anything they wanted to take; they can take it because these businesses have insurance.'*

That is the oldest criminal justification on the books. All criminals who cheat and steal, who break into businesses and rob others, all claim it's okay because only the insurance companies will suffer. It is the same **'blame the insurance company'** innuendo used to denigrate bail bonding agents. These organizations, often funded by millionaire and billionaire instigators, love to claim others are greedy; as they leave the businesses they have looted, their arms overflowing with stolen goods, a smile splitting their face.

Unfortunately for the honest citizens of California, California's legislature recently passed SB10. Career criminals are celebrating in the streets! With a new law that stipulates a 12-hour timeline from arrest to release, these criminals will be back on the streets before the police can finish their arrest reports. Criminals have scored a significant victory, Freedom without accountability! Get arrested? No sweat, you'll be back on the streets in time for supper and the next heist.

What about the victims and public safety?

What about them?

Chapter 3: He called the court to say, 'I won't be coming.' - Understanding the System
A True Story

He was a kickboxer with an attitude who had collected a series of arrests for various traffic violations and misdemeanor crimes. His current DUI case, accompanied by multiple failures to appear in court, raised his new charges' seriousness. His bond amount reflected his attitude toward society and the court system: the court set his bail amount at $25,000.

A 'bail' is a means whereby someone is released from jail after their arrest, on an agreement that they will return to court at times set until the charge for which they were arrested and charged is resolved.

Keeping in character, the criminal suspect decided that appearing in court was not going to happen. However, rather than simply failing to show up for his hearing, this defendant chose to give the court fair notice of his non-attendance by informing them they could start without him. He would not be coming.

Although the court had already been aware of this defendant's habit of non-appearances, the defendant's phone call brought a distinct new meaning to the phrase 'Contempt of Court.' Stating he would not be attending his hearing was his final slap at the system.

"Hey, I just wanted you to know that I am not coming to court. I will not be there," the defendant explained to the clerk.

The court clerk was unsure how to respond but replied, *"Is there a reason?"*

"Yea," replied the criminal suspect. *"I do not want to come. I'm moving and will not be around anymore."*

"You know they will issue a warrant for your arrest."

"Let them," the criminal suspect stated confidently.

This defendant knew the truth. Even after issuing a warrant for his arrest, it was unlikely anyone would bother coming after him. He planned to move his family down to Arizona. Once out of the state, this man believed he would be home free.

Why? His charge involved a misdemeanor DUI, and the defendant knew Colorado would not extradite him once he left the state. Out of state, his drinking and driving would no longer be an issue. Let someone else pay the penalty for his criminal behavior. He would not.

However, before he packed his bags and his family into their SUV and left the state, he made one critical error. He hadn't been allowed a bond via the Colorado Pretrial Release program. If he had, he would have been free indeed. Instead, he was required to post bail.

Why would a bail-bonding agent post a $25,000 bond for a problem defendant who clearly showed he could not be trusted? The suspect's wife worked as a court clerk and *swore* she would guarantee his next court appearance. However, the only thing she ended up making sure of was that their belongings were packed and ready to go before the court issued a warrant for her husband's arrest for failing to appear in court.

And so, after he called the court to inform them of his non-appearance, he loaded up his kids, his wife, and went on the run in America.

'Come on, kids; we're moving! I'm going to show you how to deal with the court after an arrest for drinking and driving.' His belief that freedom was one state line away drove him to load up his family and wave goodbye to Colorado.

In America, an individual arrested for any crime is considered innocent until proven guilty in a court of law. Of course, the concept does not mean the individual is genuinely innocent. It merely allows the defendant the benefit of the doubt. It is then up to the District Attorney's office to present a case that can show the defendant's guilt before the defendant can be found guilty *if* the defendant can be found guilty.

This idea of innocent until proven guilty is a fundamental right given to us by our Constitution. Because of this right, a person arrested for almost any crime has *a right to bail.* They have a right to be released from jail between court dates under the conditions outlined by the statutes dealing with bail in each state.

However, in cases of violence and specific Federal charges, the right to bail is denied. There are other times when the bail's monetary amount is so high; the defendant will not make bail. A court then denies bail through a process of exorbitant bail-setting. Exorbitant bail-setting is often the case in murder trials when a court orders the defendant held on a million-dollar bond or higher.

If every individual arrested and released from jail after their arrest failed to appear in court, there would no longer be any need to have a court.

When an individual refuses to appear in court and chooses to go on the run, they have determined that the police, the courts, and society as a whole, are irrelevant; they have, by their actions, lifted themselves above the rights of others and above the justice system designed to protect those rights. By rejecting society's right to justice, these individuals have become the most dangerous of criminals. Because they have no fear of facing the consequences of their actions, they do not need to change or alter their actions. In many cases, all they need is a state line.

The key that unlocks commercial bail's importance is *accountability,* which guarantees that an individual *will* appear in court. When a criminal suspect, arrested for a crime and released from jail after that arrest, fails to appear in court, the first crack in the justice system appears. When a defendant obtains their release via a bail-bonding agent, the bail-bonding agent guarantees the individual will appear in court as the court ordered.

When the individual arrested is released via a state-run Pretrial operation, no one is required to guarantee they will appear in court. The detained individual only promises they will show up to court. However, their promise is within the realm of their control. They can guarantee today and break that promise tomorrow. To gain their release from jail, criminal suspects always claim they will show up for court, yet many do not.

A bail-bonding agent's responsibility to the court is to locate, arrest, and return the defendant who failed to appear in court or pay the bond's amount to the court. It is a system of accountability that assures the court of the defendant's presence one way or another. Commercial bail then acts as one of the foundations of the justice system. A commercial bail bonding agent becomes an arm of the court, albeit a private one.

The idea of demanding bail while simultaneously upholding the concept of innocence until proven guilty is not a contradictory requirement placed unfairly on the individual arrested. Although a detained individual is, in the eyes of the law, considered innocent until proven guilty, the assumption that the individual may be guilty must also be viewed as a possible reality.

Commercial bail's truth and purpose are the assurance that someone will appear in court after their release from jail.

A bail-bonding program with no accountability or responsibility to assure a defendant's appearance in court is like hiring a lifeguard who can't swim to watch over the swimming pool.

Commercial bail-bonding then is one of the foundations of the justice system. Commercial bail is an integral part of the justice system in any state where it operates. As a viable part of that system, it is one of its foundational supports, assuring that the justice system works and functions with credibility.

The justice system's design is to ensure a just society, where citizens are safe and can go about their day with minimal fear of being robbed, attacked, raped, or having to encounter those who would wish them harm. In ensuring that, the justice system has a responsibility to pursue at least the following:

1. The investigation and apprehension of individuals suspected of committing a crime or violating any law;
2. Securing any individual arrested as a suspect in a crime or for a violation of any law;
3. Utilizing a method of release from jail that can assure an incarcerated defendant's appearance in court after their release;
4. The prosecution of the individual arrested while simultaneously safeguarding the suspect's rights;
5. The ongoing protection of the victim or victims who suffered from the suspect's criminal act;
6. The safeguarding of society through crime prevention, and as needed, incarceration.

If the defendant fails to appear in court, there is no longer any justice and, therefore, no active or credible justice system. A justice system without a defendant has no purpose.

The Justice System—Initiating Punishment and Change

To ensure justice and initiate change, the justice system incorporates punishment and rehabilitation as elements within its courts. These elements act as a combined power to change criminal behavior. People who develop criminal behavior patterns are highly unlikely to alter their habits if they have no compelling reason to change. When a defendant's conduct works for them, why should they change? If a thief finds it easier to steal another person's money than to earn an honest living, why should he or she get a job? Why would a drunk driver change their drinking and driving patterns if, after they are stopped, arrested, and released from jail, they are never required to answer for their actions?

An individual who cannot control their anger and acts out in violence toward another, to subjugate them to their will, has no reason to change if their actions always reap the intent of their threat, without fear of repercussions.

Punishment

Because the justice system understands that individuals will typically require an incentive to change that is greater than the rewards they receive for their harmful and criminal behavior, the justice system prepares these incentives. The system is stacked with a set of penalties, repercussions, and punishments that an individual will face if they violate the law, are caught, arrested, and convicted in a court of law. When an arrestee determines that not appearing in court can allow him or her the freedom to avoid these penalties, punishments, and repercussions, a temptation to run is born.

If their refusal to appear in a courtroom will have little to no consequence and no fear of capture, what good is the law they violated that caused their arrest? When statutes violated, and the system for dealing with those violations can be ignored through non-appearance, what value does the system have?

Rehabilitation

Another aspect of the justice system is rehabilitation. While the justice system, through the courts, hands down a sentence of punishments and penalties to anyone convicted of a crime, it is understood that encouraging a defendant's change with positive enforcement is also a good idea. To punish without rehabilitation is not enough. To send the same criminal convicted and punished for a crime back onto the streets without any ability to cope differently than before their arrest will, undoubtedly, bring about the same results; another crime will be committed.

No rehabilitation assures a state and the community where the ex-con lives that there will be new victims. For this reason, a court will add rehabilitation into the mix of punishments and penalties. The thought is based on the hope that:

a. The sentence will cause fear, the penalties a heavy, unwanted burden, and;
b. The rehabilitation will be a light at the end of the tunnel.

However, in this entire process, the most essential and valuable commodity is the defendant and his or her action of appearing in court. If the defendant fails to appear in court, all the punishments and penalties a court could order, and all the world-renowned behavioral modification programs a court can come up with are worthless.

If a person bases their behavior on what works for them and can get away with not appearing in court, there will be no behavioral change. If a person enjoys drinking and driving yet does not show up for court after an arrest, will they alter their behavior? If a defendant, twice convicted for a DUI, knows he can drive across a state line with no fear of court or of being arrested, free from punishment and penalties, will he stick around for court? Many do not.

When an individual arrested and charged with a DUI gets in their car and drives across the state line, the only one who will go after that fleeing suspect, if anyone, is a bail-bonding agent or a fugitive recovery agent.

Commercial bail's value is in a bail bonding agent's ability to assure the defendants' appearance in court. That court appearance then secures the very foundation of the justice system, set up to protect society.

A court can free the innocent and sentence the guilty. However, if no defendant appears in court, the court can do little except issue another warrant.

Critics of commercial bail-bonding often like to have it both ways. On the one hand, they state that a bail-bonding agent arresting and returning a fugitive is not justice. It is only about money. We would note that the concept of money is the same reason Colorado *will not* actively pursue each offender on the run. The costs of chasing down and extraditing every fugitive that crosses a state line are prohibitive for the state of Colorado or any other state. That is why the Colorado State Legislature, in their wisdom, saw the value of commercial bail as a support system to the courts. It is a support system with accountability to ensure a defendant's court appearance.

Critics also like to mock the concept of a bail-bonding agent's pursuit of justice in tracking, arresting, and returning a fugitive to face prosecution. These critics claim that without the bail-bonding agent, the criminal would have never been released from jail in the first place. Of course, this is a patently nonsensical argument since these same critics are the ones who call for the freeing of all criminal suspects without any bail. Those who oppose bail bonding prefer criminal suspects each have a *Crime-for-Free* Bond.

When a criminal suspect is on the run from a commercial bail bondsman, someone is in pursuit. The end of that pursuit is justice, justice for the bail-bonding agent, justice for the victim, and justice for the citizens who are victimized by these fugitives. As stated previously, *at times, a bail-bonding agent or fugitive recovery agent is a victim's last hope for justice.*

The concept of Pretrial release is that the taxpayers should pay the cost of bail services to anyone arrested as a suspect in a crime. Because arrestees are all innocent, they should not be kept in jail. They should all be freed. And it is the citizens of the state, the victimized, who should now pay the suspect's bail. The *Catch and Release* methods set up by Pretrial operations across the country are a criminal's preferred option of release from jail. In a *Catch and Release* system, a criminal has little fear of arrest. They have the assurance that their detention is no more than a minor inconvenience. The criminal suspect also agrees that innocent citizens should bear the cost of that inconvenience.

To let everyone out on a *Crime-for-Free* program on the premise that sounds noble is not grounded. It is a dangerous escalation in the freeing of criminal suspects. Allowing an individual arrested as a suspect in a potential crime to determine whether they will appear in court allows the defendant to control the justice system.

Without a defendant, the court has no purpose. Without a means of securing and assuring the defendant's appearance in court, in a manner that includes accountability and responsibility, a suspect's appearance in court is nothing more than a crapshoot based on the promises of those whose life is a con.

Failing to appear in court, for many, is a practiced and well-informed decision. This information on how to run, where to run, and even when to run is common knowledge known and shared by criminals when they are arrested and jailed. The inmates all have a common bond. They are all innocent. That they are all in jail is someone else's fault. Their imprisonment then becomes an educational facility that facilitates learning, where the teachers are the prisoners themselves, who hold the secrets of their trade. And they easily and readily share the secrets of that trade with one another. That trade is the ability to avoid arrest and detection. Their education begins after their arrest. Their fellow prisoners, the teachers, teach how to use Pretrial's unique *Catch and Release* Program to their advantage. The teaching reviews correct answers and excuses that work well in interviews with Pretrial and in court. Inmates guide each other on how to answer Pretrial's questions to gain the confidence of those who can recommend their release with a signature and a promise to appear. And once they obtain their freedom on a *Crime-for-Free* Bond, they are FREE INDEED!

Concerning a commercial bond, inmates play the same game. However, because bail agents are accountable and responsible for the defendant's appearance in court, the agents know the game well. They have become the real experts in bail. Even though bail-bonding agents may, at times, also fall victim to a criminal suspect's game, the agents will either find and seek out the fugitive or be required to pay a financial penalty.

In California, several counties employ a dangerous computer-generated algorithm within their Pretrial assessment. They claim these algorithms are scientifically accurate and can determine an arrested individual's risk factors if released from jail. This algorithm claims to know if a criminal suspect will go to court or present a danger to society once freed. It is the computer genius of the bail reform movement.

However, it is essential to note that these algorithms are nothing more than computer-generated questionnaires created by men and women who enter data into a computer to come up with the computer's guess-work analysis and freedom assessment.

The algorithms are based on what men and women decide to input into the computer. These computer assessments then produce questionnaires filled out by pretrial assessment personnel and the criminal suspects wanting out of jail. At this point, just like high school, a score is given. If the score falls within the computer's good guy, good gal, you're okay, I'm OK category, the criminal suspect passes and is awarded his or her freedom.

That these computer algorithms hold scientific value at all is a matter of debate.

In San Francisco, one case challenges brainy computer algorithms; the release of a criminal suspect named Mims in 2017. The Algorithm claimed this defendant had a low offender score; in other words, his release from jail, pending court, held little or no risk to society. Of course, that did not help Mr. Edward French; he was murdered after the defendant was freed from jail. Mims and his partner selected Mr. French as a perfect victim for a robbery.

In defense of their Algorithm, those running the Pretrial assessment program for the court stated that it was an error of addition that allowed for Mims' easy release. What was the mistake? Pretrial claimed one of their workers entered an incorrect number of days that Mims was previously incarcerated. Entering the wrong number of days gave Mims a low rating and awarded him his release. It was just a math error. Well, golly gee.

This excuse would be hilarious if it weren't so tragic. Mims was sitting in jail on new charges of parole violation and possession of a firearm after multiple previous convictions. It does not take a rocket scientist or a flawed computer-generated algorithm trying to calculate how many days he was previously incarcerated to know that releasing him would be a bad idea. Any individual with common sense would have known better than to allow this man's release.

Regarding his release, the judge hearing his case gave a nice sound bite claiming Mims was to be released with '***assertive case management***.' This is a Pretrial program that requires check-ins. That worked out real nice for everyone except for Mr. French, Mims' victim following his algorithm release.

Supporters of this scary computer program claim that it offers 'validated, evidence-based data' to make a sound decision. Really? The real evidence and data all suggested Mr. Mims was dangerous. A computer program wasn't required to make this assessment. He was a felon arrested on a Parole violation and in possession of a firearm. What about that being a dangerous combination did anyone not see?

The outcome of this failure was a dangerous felon on the streets and a dead seventy-one-year-old man, a professional photographer. And this is the glaring cover-up of bail reform. The one word they never mention while raising their voice on behalf of the arrested is the word, 'Victim.' The only victim in the reform movement is the criminal suspect, unfairly detained and jailed.

Where there is no court, there is no justice. Where there is no justice, there is only anarchy. And anarchy is the crumbling of a society that chooses not to care about its victims or the citizens it is obliged to protect. We currently see that anarchy on the streets of Seattle, Portland, Chicago, New York, and other cities where bail reform has taken root, to the delight of those who burn and loot, threaten others, shoot and stab, and now demand the defunding of the police. Pure lawlessness under the covers of justice. If only someone would give them a loaf of bread!

In the earlier fugitive case, who called the court to say he would not show, the bail-bonding agent who posted the bond was not ready to concede. He was not prepared to allow the fugitive his freedom so easily.

Soon after the bonded man moved his family out of the State of Colorado, the bail-bonding agent contacted a fugitive recovery agent. A brief investigation led the recovery agent to believe the fugitive had run off to Arizona. The fugitive recovery agent packed his bags and headed south.

The agent chasing the runner arrived in Phoenix approximately a month after the criminal suspect. His plan then had to be blended into the laws of the state of Arizona. When any state's statutes appear to hinder a fugitive recovery agent's operational ability, the agent must think outside of the box to capture and return his runner. With his authority limited in Arizona, this recovery agent proceeded as a private insurance investigator and began with a stealth operation.

In Colorado, bail-bonding agents are licensed, insurance agents. When anyone involved with signing contracts or being released on a bond violates those contracts, their actions can be considered insurance fraud. For this reason, a few recovery agents specialize in insurance fraud. As insurance investigators, these individuals investigate frauds perpetrated by anyone signing bail contracts or those who go on the run while on bail. They have a 'Power to Arrest' given by the bail-bonding agent having custody of the defendant.

These agents often operate in stealth mode, watching and investigating at a distance. There are no block searches in a stealth investigation, pounding on neighborhood doors, and flashing the criminal suspect's picture, hoping for a lead. One wrong move, and the fugitive could run again.

The first address the agent staked out required three days of investigative time to determine that the criminal suspect was not living there. His researcher in Denver then came up with a second address.

Without adequate research support, a fugitive recovery agent can be left empty on ideas and plans once they arrive in the field of operation. In Phoenix, a large metro area that includes Mesa, Tempe, and other adjoining suburban centers, a search needs to be focused and isolated. One cannot hit the streets, driving around aimlessly, hoping that the criminal suspect will appear by chance.

On day four, the fugitive recovery agent received a new address lead and completed a neighborhood overview and drive-by. The home was in a cul-de-sac and not situated in a place conducive to quiet observation. To attempt a direct approach could be extremely dangerous. If the fugitive were not at home, the investigator's visit would act as a warning bell. If the criminal suspect was at home, the question of force could be problematic. The agent knew the fugitive had two small children, and, in this case, safety was of prime importance. The positive news was that the vehicle spotted in the suspect residence's driveway matched the family's vehicle description.

In Arizona, a fugitive recovery agent from another state is prohibited from arresting and removing a fugitive against his will unless the agent first hires a local, licensed fugitive recovery agent to assist with the arrest. Unless the Colorado agent could confirm the culprit was at home, there was no purpose in hiring the local help.

The agent mapped out the neighborhood for most likely entrances and exits. He also made a run through the nearby business district for possible shopping outlets that could draw the fugitive and his family. After all, they would need to go shopping. They had to eat something! After selecting two optimal locations from which to spot vehicles coming to and leaving from the neighborhood, the agent set up surveillance.

Surveillance is not a simple game of waiting in a car, eating, drinking, and reading the newspaper or a good book. It is a tedious and straining activity that stretches one's patience to the extreme. To look away in one instant, at the wrong time, can mean your suspect has passed right by, and you are none the wiser. It only takes a minute of unfocused awareness to destroy an entire operation.

And so, times were selected, and the waiting began. The early morning, before people left for work, was prime time. A drive through the neighborhood, a view of the home, a brief park on the side, then off again.

A gas station, a block up from the residential community, appeared to be a good morning watchpoint. It sat on the edge of the main thoroughfare leading to a highway that circumvented the entire Phoenix metro area. A rumor was circulating that the defendant's wife worked as a court clerk or in a law firm in the Phoenix area. The most practical way for her to head from her residence in the morning was right by the station along the highway.

The Agent arose before the sun, drove to his designated spot, parked, and waited. He waited one day, then two. Then on the third day, as his thoughts began to wonder, the defendant's wife's vehicle entered the gas station right in front of him, pulled up to the pump, and filled her tank. The agent watched, hoping for an opportunity to follow her vehicle.

After she completed her gas purchase, she pulled out of the station. The agent paused and then followed two cars behind. Up ahead, the female caught a green turn light. The agent did not. Losing hope, the agent watched her drive off only to see her get caught at the next red light. Optimism surged as his light turned green. And so, it went all the way to the highway onramp. She would get through a light; he would get stuck. Then up ahead, she would catch her own red light while his would turn green. It was a traffic light game of hopscotch.

However, the final blow was when the agent believed the woman had spotted him, so he had to turn off the road into a strip mall. By the time he got back onto the street, she was on the ramp to the highway, racing off towards downtown Phoenix. Although he tried to catch up, racing along at breakneck speeds was neither a safe nor right approach to tailing a fugitive or his family. At all times, consideration for safety must rise above desire. The defendant's wife disappeared into the ever-growing morning metallic herd of traffic.

That day another lead arrived, suggesting the fugitive was working at a home repair outlet. The agent reviewed several home repair establishments in the area and selected the most probable. He then contacted a local fugitive recovery agent. If the agent came along as a backup, the Arizona agent would receive $200 for accompanying him to stay within the law's restraints. The payoff would take place after the defendant's successful arrest. But the Arizona agent did not like that deal. He wanted $200 just to show up; whether the defendant was there was irrelevant. The proposal was unacceptable to the investigating agent.

With several home repair stores in the area and a couple in the communities next door, just paying these guys $200 every time he went to a new store would get costly. Unfortunately, there is no magical brotherhood of fugitive recovery agents. These guys did not want to go anywhere without a sure payout. If they were not guaranteed a payoff, they weren't getting off the couch. Fortunately, Colorado fugitive recovery agents seem to have a little more ambition and drive. They go out with no guarantees.

The investigation dragged on with days of drive-bys and visits to local home repair businesses.

On the ninth day of the operation, the fugitive recovery agent visited a local print store, designed a wanted poster, and printed a dozen copies. Having no success in stealth mode, he had run out of viable options. The investigation went active. The agent began a systematic elimination of each worksite where the fugitive could be employed. At each store, the agent would request a manager and show them the wanted poster. However, the answer was always the same: none of them knew the fugitive in the picture.

Before leaving Colorado, the agent had read up on the Arizona statutes forbidding an arrest and forceful removal of any fugitive from the state without in-state agent help. However, a conversation he had one evening with a local police officer was encouraging.

On that night, during a conversation with a police officer he met, the agent explained his dilemma. The officer replied that an option might be a citizen's arrest. Arizona *did* allow for a citizen's arrest. This suggestion put a new card in play, and the agent doubled down on his search.

His researcher then informed the agent that this fugitive had a warrant out of Maricopa County, Arizona. Maricopa County of the famed Arizona Tent City Jail and inmates with pink underwear was not a favorite for criminals.

On the thirteenth day of the operation, the insurance investigator began to wonder if he should turn the whole affair over to local law enforcement. He was fearful he could wait for weeks without spotting the fugitive, and time was running out. However, because police stations close to the public after five and it was after hours, the investigator decided to wait until morning.

Back at his staging area, making his cursory drive through the fugitive's neighborhood, he blinked. As the investigator turned into the cul-de-sac, the fugitive's vehicle drove right past him, going in the opposite direction. The criminal suspect's wife and child were with him, but they failed to notice the surprised expression on the driver of the vehicle they were passing.

The agent pulled into the neighborhood, made a U-turn, and raced back out onto the main road. He spotted the fugitive stopped at a red light in a turning lane and was able to get one car behind the defendant. He waited.

This time the agent did not catch the red light. He followed the fugitive the few blocks up the street until the family's SUV turned into a strip mall. Following them, the agent observed the family exit their vehicle and watched as they entered a Goodwill store. The agent retrieved his cuffs and left the car. He would arrest the criminal suspect in the store.

When affecting an arrest, safety is always one of the primary considerations. However, no arrest is ever risk-free, no matter the preparations. An arrest, by the very nature of the act, is risky. The location of the arrest often determines safety and risk. In this instance, although the first thought is one of danger, the procedure mastered by the insurance investigator would assure no one else would be hurt. The agent carried no weapons, just a pair of cuffs. And the store, a public place, could be the safest place to take down this kickboxing fugitive from Colorado.

The agent entered the store and began a slow walk into and among the menswear. He spotted the criminal proceeding through two racks of clothes, came upon him, grabbed his hand, and greeted him with a "Hi."

The fugitive was startled and began to tense, but not before the agent slapped one handcuff on the target's right wrist and one cuff on his own hand. In less than three seconds, the investigator had secured the fugitive.

"You have an outstanding warrant, and I'm making a citizen's arrest." The agent stated. He observed the fugitive begin to stress out, his eyes darting about from his cuffs to any possible escape route. There were none. For the criminal to run, he would have to drag the agent along with him.

"Look," said the agent in a firm but soft voice, "If I wanted you to go to jail, I would have this store crawling with police. I have a warrant for your arrest out of Colorado, but I think we can talk this out if you cooperate. If not, you will go to jail on multiple charges too numerous to count. And you will not get out anytime soon."

"So, let's talk," said the fugitive.

"Outside," the agent replied. "We go outside very calmly, and then we will talk." The agent threw a jacket over the cuffs and walked with the fugitive out of the front doors. The fugitive's family followed them out.

Once outside, the fugitive spoke first. "Okay, let's talk."

"First, I need to put you in a secured custody," said the agent, pulling the second set of cuffs from his pocket. "Put your free arm behind your back." When the fugitive hesitated, the agent added, "Look, comply or go straight to jail. I don't care which."

The fugitive put his free hand behind his back, and the agent could cuff him properly. "We are going to walk to my car, and then we will talk."

At the vehicle, the recovery agent positioned the fugitive with his back to the transport vehicle's rear door, pulled out a set of shackles connected to the transport, and shackled him. It was only then that the investigator was able to breathe a sigh of relief. The fugitive was adequately handcuffed and chained to his vehicle. He wasn't going anywhere.

"Okay, you said we could talk," the fugitive said.

"And we will," replied the agent, who retrieved a video recorder and stand, which he set up and turned on. The agent stated for the camera who he was and that he had just made a citizen's arrest on a fugitive who had a warrant out of Maricopa County in Arizona and one out of Colorado.

"So, here's the deal," stated the agent, turning the video camera to shoot the fugitive's reply. "You have a warrant out of Maricopa County and one out of Colorado. What do you want to do? Would you prefer I take you to Maricopa County Jail, or are you willing to voluntarily return with me to Colorado?"

The fugitive was now resigned to his fate. But rather than be taken to Maricopa County Jail and remain in Arizona, he chose to return to Colorado.

"So, you are choosing to return to Colorado with me of your own free will. Is that correct?" the agent asked.

"Yes," replied the fugitive.

The agent swung the camera around to the fugitive's wife. "Are you a witness to the fact that your husband has requested I return him to Colorado and that he has made this request of his own free will?"

"Yes," answered the wife.

"Great! Then I guess it's back to Colorado," the agent said, who then loaded the fugitive into the vehicle's back seat.

I guess guys do not like pink underwear!

Was this arrest—in a store, in front of his family—a safe one? Yes. It was the safest arrest for this individual at that time. The recovery agent carried no weapon, so no one else would have been harmed if the fugitive had fought the recovery agent. As a kickboxer, this runner wasn't shy about his ability to defend himself.

For these reasons, the agent had used a soft arrest technique that required speed and focus. He approached and cuffed the fugitive before the fugitive's brain could react to what was happening. The agent operated in that split second of uncertainty where the mind clouds, unable to act or comprehend what's going on. By the time the fugitive had realized what had happened, there was nothing he could do. Once handcuffed, there was no way he could make a break. Here he was in a public place, his kids and wife watching, and he was cuffed and arrested, told they could work it out. What other choice did he have? None.

This approach is not standard for every fugitive recovery agent, but as an experienced agent, who profiled and tracked fugitives, this was this agent's safest move. Nobody was hurt, and the arrest was over in seconds.

Even outside the store, the agent moved the fugitive along to his car, ever talking, reassuring, manipulating this fugitive to a place of safety: in shackles with the fugitive's hands cuffed behind his back.

These are low-level, soft approach arrests that allow for quick, close-up contact with the fugitive before they can think enough to run.

However, these types of arrests should never be attempted by anyone not experienced and proficient at understanding and operating in fast, close-quarter scenarios.

In the vehicle, the fugitive made two comments.

Statement one: "What just happened?"

To which the agent replied, "You were arrested."

Statement two: "I didn't think anyone would come for me."

This fugitives' statement once again confirmed the truth: offenders believe no one will come for them. However, when even one runner is caught and returned to justice, the word spreads, and everyone else in the jail now knows that if they do not go to court, they are not home free. If they are on a commercial bail bond and run, someone is coming for them. That alone can dissuade a criminal suspect from crossing the state line. If, when they run, they are going to get caught and returned to face justice, they might just as well go to court now.

On the trip back to Colorado, the fugitive did make one additional off-handed remark. "You know," began the culprit, "if I had wanted to, I could have thrown you off and taken you down with a kick."

"Yea," replied the agent. "Well, I'm grateful you didn't."

The truth of the fugitive's last statement lay buried beneath the fact that the arrest had happened so fast, the target did not have time to think, react, or do anything but get cuffed. There was no warning notice.

The arrogant fugitive who had told the court he was not coming to court was still arrogant. Now, regaining his composure, he pictured himself throwing the agent to the ground with a punch and a kick and a... *'Oh well, not this time.'*

And always, the hope is that one who understands they will not escape the consequences of their actions may then finally decide to change their actions. They may not. But at least they have the opportunity.

And that is the strength of commercial bail and fugitive recovery. If this man had been out on a Pretrial bond, he would have still been in Arizona, laughing at the Colorado justice system and how he had told the court he would not appear. Then he could again drink and drive until his next arrest or until he broadsided an innocent family while cruising down the road drunk.

Now he understands there are consequences to drinking and driving, and you cannot run and hide after being arrested.

Chapter 4: New Mexico Proclaims Freedom
The Trojan Horse

Amalia, New Mexico

During an investigation into a missing three-year-old boy from Georgia, law enforcement officials raided a desert compound near Amalia, New Mexico. Police officers discovered the remains of a dead boy and eleven other malnourished children living in squalor with no running water or electricity on the compound. Before the raid, the sheriff's department and police had stated they had intercepted a message from the compound asking for help: **We are starving and need food and water.**

Law enforcement secured a search warrant and raided the compound. Besides the eleven children living in squalid conditions, they also discovered a rich cache of weapons, including an AR-15 and a Glock, both locked and loaded. The search also uncovered a shooting range, and documents law enforcement alleged showed the adults within the compound were training and planning for armed acts of violence. The dead boy's body was the missing child from Georgia, illegally taken from his mother's legal custody.

After arresting the five adults and turning over the freed children to Child-Protective Services, one child testified that their own training included how to shoot up a school.

The adults who had moved onto the property and set up their primitive makeshift compound said they thought the property they lived on was theirs. However, the property owners stated they had told the adults several times that they were not allowed on the property. The adults were not tenants. They did not pay rent. They were squatters—armed and dangerous squatters—that the owners had repeatedly attempted to kick off their land.

Within a week of their arrest, three of the five had been released on New Mexico's new favored bail reform laws, and charges were dismissed.

Before releasing three of the five, one judge stated there was not enough evidence to hold the group in jail as being dangerous to society. The judge's statement bore a lame horse's credibility in the Kentucky Derby, hoping to win a trifecta. They were arrested while squatting on private property. With them were eleven starving children and a weapons stash with loaded firearms. The property also yielded the dead body of a three-year-old boy who had been illegally taken from his mother in Georgia and moved across state lines. The boys' body was discovered buried on the property. One would seem to think the combining circumstances equaled a bit of danger, wouldn't one?

Although there was a public outcry, the judge simply recited New Mexico laws that dealt with individuals held in jail on bail. One judge blamed prosecutors for failing to meet a ten-day deadline required by the law. Another judge claimed she could not see any evidence that would lead her to believe that releasing these individuals would threaten anyone. Perhaps they were not a threat anyone else, but what of the dead child and eleven starving, malnourished, barefooted children, dressed in rags, living in poverty in a makeshift desert home with no electricity, plumbing, or running water and a playground of broken bottles, filth, and trash?

This investigation and the arrest of the five adults occurred in 2018. Their arrest and release made front-page news and was given prime-time attention on cable outlets. TV channels appeared to promote the goodness of the adults arrested and lambasted crazed attitudes of those enraged by the judge's releasing three of the five.

However, in 2019, all five were indicted by a federal grand jury in Albuquerque. Their charges were terror-related, alleging a conspiracy to provide material support for terrorist attacks on federal officers and employees, transporting a child illegally across state lines, and various other acts contrary to lawful conduct. A grand jury is a group of citizens who review the evidence presented by a district attorney. These citizens are not law enforcement specialists; just everyday people called out to make an unbiased decision on the evidence showed.

How thankful we should be that regular people, off the streets, can hear evidence presented and, using common sense, come to a reasonable opinion. It shows that citizens prefer justice over *Crime-for-Free*, out on whim rulings by judges who are clueless or have their own secret agendas.

The adults indicted are currently in custody. We can now also be thankful; New Mexico Bail Reform has not yet trickled into the Federal Judiciary.

Today, as a movement falsely called Bail Reform sweeps across the country, one should take heed of the saying, 'Beware of strangers bearing gifts.'

The original saying states, 'Beware of Greeks bearing gifts' and was a Greek mythology product and the Trojan Horse story. A history lesson taught at school, a movie made with Brad Pitt, many have heard the Trojan Horse tale.

Having gathered an army of Greeks, a king named Agamemnon set forth to reclaim a lady called Helen. As the Greeks camped outside Troy's walls, a ten-year siege followed, but the Greeks could not breach Troy's secured walls.

Then one day, a brilliant idea emerged. The Greeks built a giant, hollow, wooden horse. At night, they filled the hollow of the horse with armed men. Then they rolled the horse up to the gates of Troy and retreated out of sight. To the viewers on the walls of Troy, it appeared that the Greeks had sailed away. They had not.

Early the next morning, the watchers on Troy's walls looked out onto an empty battlefield but for one large wooden horse. Had the enemy fled, worn out by the long siege? And in their stead, the Greeks had left behind a gift of acknowledgment to the victors—the Horse?

Troy celebrated, opened the gates, and rolled in the wooden Horse. The entire day was an extended celebration of victory, with Trojans feasting and drinking their way into oblivion.

However, that night, exhausted from eating and drinking—a day with great joy—they quickly fell fast asleep. As they slept, the Horse awakened, and from within the hollow emerged Greek warriors who destroyed the city and murdered its inhabitants.

And so, the saying 'Beware of Greeks bearing gifts' emerged and later became 'Beware of strangers bearing gifts.'

Is Bail Reform nothing more than a Trojan Horse? Should we beware of others who claim they are bearing gifts of justice?

In 2016, New Mexico voters approved bail reform in their state. After a campaign of high and noble promises, the citizens voted to allow a non-profit Trojan Horse, The Arnold Foundation, to step in and overthrow the bail-bonding industry with its own specially designed assessment tool. However, this tool is nothing more than a computer-generated question and answer form.

The bail reform campaign is a shadow of The Arnold Foundation's intent to bulldoze through the bail-bonding industry without accountability. Their plan to abolish commercial bail is at the victims' expense, who they ignored without thought or care.

How has this worked out for New Mexico? One only needs to go to YouTube, where the previous governor of New Mexico laments about this movement's destruction and threat.

The previous governor of New Mexico, Susana Martinez, now warns other states before they too look out across their state line and see the enormous Trojan Horse waiting as a trophy of victory. Governor Martinez warns others of the suspect criminals hiding within the horse, criminals who wholeheartedly support their unaccountable quick release after each arrest.

The New Mexico Governor's YouTube message begins with the title, '**A Special Message from New Mexico Governor Susana**

Martinez.' She then describes the disastrous results of bail reform and the Arnold Foundations assessment tool:

> **Good morning. I'm Suzanna Martinez, Governor of New Mexico. Before taking office, I was a prosecutor for 25 years. Keeping dangerous criminals off the streets and behind bars where they belong has always been one of my top priorities. As leaders in Utah work to consider reforms to bail bonds and Pretrial detention release, I know your top priority is to keep your citizens safe from dangerous and repeat criminals.**
>
> **Here in New Mexico, we've been working hard to crack down on a *Catch and Release*, revolving door criminal justice system. A problem that irresponsible interpretations and rules implemented by courts and the *Arnold Pretrial risk assessment tool has only aggravated.***
>
> **New Mexico implemented this Pretrial risk assessment tool to devastating results. I encourage those in Utah to be very skeptical of voices calling for misleading devices that would result in letting dangerous criminals back out on the street to terrorize communities.**
>
> **Thank you for your time, and God bless you as you move forward in working to make your state a safer place.**

Next on the bail reform hit list, this governor makes a plea with Utah to listen to the lessons New Mexico has learned as they attempt to crack down on their new *Catch and Release*, revolving door, criminal-justice system. Through court rulings and, as she points out, the fraudulent Arnold Foundation Pretrial Assessment Tool, their state has suffered the consequences. The Foundation's Assessment Tool frees criminals and, with a *Crime-for-Free* bond, puts them back on the streets as quickly as they are arrested. Who needs accountability when Arnold's in town?

The Governor goes on to explain that New Mexico implemented this new Pretrial Assessment Tool with devastating results. She warns others to beware of misleading devices that promise justice but are no more than the crime for free, *Catch and Release* systems that offer no accountability.

As the Trojan Horse loomed huge as a gift of victory to the watchers on the walls of Troy, so do The Arnold Foundation, and their Pre-trial Assessment Tool loom large as a picture-perfect victory for justice. However, as many in New Mexico now believe, the Trojan Horse wheeled into their state contained nothing more than a process for quickly releasing the criminal suspects lurking within the hollow of the Horse, as everyone sleeps.

As they pushed their assessment tool as a win-win for bail reform, many in New Mexico discovered it was no more than a win-win for criminals. Criminals now have no fear of arrest. They have the assurance of a quick release and freedom at the expense of those they violated, the citizens of New Mexico.

While the Arnold Foundation has pushed its algorithm as the scientific gold mine to analyze and classify those arrested, it is the law-abiding citizen who suffers. And the head of the Arnold Foundation, John Arnold, has plenty of experience watching hard-working men and women suffer.

In 2001, as Enron was preparing to file bankruptcy, it was not that long ago that Mr. John Arnold increased his wealth. At the end of 2001, when an energy company, Enron, filed for bankruptcy, Enron's workers lost their jobs. Along with their jobs, gone were their pensions and health care coverage, for which they had worked all their lives. All vanished in the smoke of Enron's bankruptcy.

And during 2000 and 2001, where was John Arnold billionaire extraordinaire? He was leading the Enron Energy Traders on behalf of Enron. While the hard workers at Enron lost everything, Mr. Arnold was raking in millions. As David Barboza of the *New York Times* explained in 2002, '**Enron's trading unit generated the bulk of the company's profits in 2000 and 2001, and as a result, its executives and traders received a majority of the $50 million in retention bonuses the company agreed to pay just ahead of the bankruptcy filing.**'

The article also went on to state, '**The disclosure of scores of large cash payments is certain to increase the ire of former lower-level employees who have long complained about how high-level executives sold more than $1 billion in Enron shares in the year before the company filed for bankruptcy protection. Thousands of Enron workers were laid off after the filing on December 2, and many have complained they got little in severance pay and lost millions of dollars they had put into the company's 401(k) retirement accounts.'**

As one of Enron's traders, playing the market and betting on energy prices as they rose and fell, Arnold became Enron's top gun. Arnold appeared to be the master of knowing whether energy prices would rise or fall. And who, an investigation later discovered, was responsible for many of those energy fluctuations? As it turned out, Enron itself manipulated the price and cost of energy by faking shortages and causing outages. In one instance, Enron had one plant in California temporarily closed for no other purpose than to force the rise of energy prices to improve their profit margin. This illuminating discovery surfaced when the famous Enron Tapes came to light.

As Californians lost billions through energy surcharges, coached along by Enron, an investigation concluded Enron manipulated the energy crises for monetary gain. At that time, Mr. Arnold made three-quarters of a billion dollars for the company. This company would then terminate its employees, eliminate their pensions, and cancel their health care benefits.

The loss for the public in California through energy price manipulations was also extreme. Enron's actions at deceit and manipulations exasperated the California Energy Crises in 2000 and 2001. This energy crisis caused California to declare a state of emergency and cost one California governor his job, according to a 2005 report by the *Guardian*.

Finally, the damage to the stockholders, who saw the value of their stock holdings fall to nothing in the fall of 2001, was a sharp contrast to Enron and Mr. Arnold's benefits during the same timeframe.

Arnold made over half a billion for Enron and pocketed eight million dollars as a bonus for himself.

And what did John Arnold have to say of his dealings and knowledge when Enron manipulated and cheated the everyday citizen? In a report regarding Testimony before the Senate Policy Committee, Robert McCullough, Manager of McCullough research, reported the following:

> **'Recently in Texas, John Arnold, Enron's most profitable trader, chose to plead the Fifth Amendment concerning the details of a single forward gas contract. Of course, Enron traders frequently take the Fifth Amendment. In this case, it is far more significant since Mr. Arnold was responsible for forward gas transactions and contributed 21% of Enron's North American earnings in 2001.'**

It seems curious that an individual can profit from the rise and fall of energy prices while working on behalf of an energy company that an investigation revealed rigged those prices.

And this is the man who now established his own foundation, pushing his newest and latest Trojan Horse into one state after another across the country. As he sits back in relative comfort, others *should* fear.

As the New Mexico governor warned, *'New Mexico implemented this Pretrial Risk assessment tool to devastating results.'* The governor then warns others *'to be very skeptical about voices calling for misleading devices that would result in letting dangerous criminals back out on the streets to terrorize communities.'* Will you now have to sit by as they roll the Horse into your state? Will you only realize the devastating effects unleashed as criminals crawl out of the hollow of the Horse while everyone else sleeps?

It took New Mexico less than two years to wake up and see the 'devasting results' of the Arnold Foundation's Trojan Horse. It is a Trojan Horse that never considers the victims or the communities' safety where the horse is left. It is a system that has absolutely no accountability.

For a first-hand account of the New Mexico Governor's YouTube message, go online and listen for yourself: <u>New Mexico Governor Takes to YouTube to Warn Utah Against Bail Reforms</u>

For a justice system to protect the public, accountability is essential. Without accountability, public safety is nothing more than a good sound bite, and victims' rights, nothing more than an afterthought.

Bail Reform, falsely called reform, focuses on freeing anyone arrested, allowing criminal suspects their freedom without any accountability. Within this morass of revolving door justice, the victim and honest citizens have been shoved aside as a nuisance.

In the final analysis, a justice system that depends on the criminal suspect to decide if they will appear in court if they feel the court is worth their time is a justice system that has begun to fall to the criminals' mercy. Why insist on accountability when we don't need it? Perhaps the courts should allow the criminal suspects to set their own court dates and show up if they have time. If they fail to appear for their court date, we can always hope they fled, crossed the state line, and are now cheating, robbing, raping, and stealing from others in a neighboring state. Let justice escape with the criminal suspects and let another state and their innocent citizens bear the burden of the fugitives hiding within their populations.

Chapter 5: He held off a swat team using his son as a shield - Monitoring Defendants
A True Story

In years past, he held off a Montana Swat Team... using his infant son as a hostage. Later he served seven years in the Colorado Department of Corrections for severely beating a woman. Now, his ex-wife was terrified. Even after twenty years apart, her fear of this man filled her with dread. He was on his way to Washington State, to her home area.

In a panic, she called the Denver Police Department. She reported that this man, who once used her son as a hostage, had cut off an ankle monitor and was on his way to Spokane. He was coming to the area she now called home.

The Denver Police Department stated that there was nothing they could do. They explained that his new crime, the crime of domestic violence, the reason the defendant was required to wear the monitor, was considered a minor offense, and they would not be going after him. They had no jurisdiction to chase down a defendant who had fled the state on a misdemeanor.

The private company that contracted with Pretrial to monitor the defendant via the electronic ankle bracelet notified Pretrial after the defendant cut off the monitor.

Pretrial, who funnels their monitoring responsibilities to private companies through exclusive contracts, may have filed a report. Still, they did not notify the police, nor did they contact anyone to check the defendant's residence. Pretrial did not reach the bail-bonding agent who had posted the bond, who did have the power to affect the defendant's arrest immediately. The Court that had ordered the defendant to wear an ankle monitor had no idea the defendant had cut off his ankle monitor and fled the State of Colorado.

No one bothered to contact the authorities in Spokane, Washington. They were not notified that a dangerous, violent man was on his way. No one called to say an ex-wife in their area was frightened for her life because this man with uncontrolled rage was on the road.

When the bail-bonding agent who posted this defendant's bail first received a call from the criminal suspect's friends, they explained that he was in jail on a $7,500 bond for domestic violence. The friends stated that the bond was high because of the extensive property damage caused by his actions. His friends also assured the bail agent that the criminal suspect was a good friend and a trustworthy individual.

Bail-bonding agents are not informed on the details of any case or given the individuals' background for whom they post bond. They often must rely on what they can gather from those who call requesting help. Although specific websites now allow for a background search, most of these searches are state-based. One must know which state the defendant was locked up in to proceed with an investigation. There are also name changes, aliases, and information received and controlled by law enforcement organizations, easily accessible to Pretrial that is not made available to bail-bonding agents.

Bail-bonding agents considering the posting of a bond, at times, only have minutes on a phone call to decide. Often, crucial information is unattainable, and events or criminal history that could provide a clearer picture are absent. For these reasons, bail bonding agents will rely on the criminal suspect's information and family. When critical information is left out, a bail agent must depend on the worthiness of those contacting him or her.

As this bail-bonding agent met with the criminal suspect's friends, who were sound citizens with a good work history and clean records, he was unaware of the dangers this man would pose once released.

A group of people knew those dangers, but the bail-bonding agent was not one of them. The people who knew were from the court and Pretrial Services, which stated they would monitor the defendant upon his release.

The court had the benefit of reviewing the defendant's past, the current charges, and the risks the Court believed he might pose. It then set the bond, accordingly, ordering Pretrial Services to monitor the defendant.

Pretrial Services decided on an extensive plan to control this defendant if he made a bond because of his past. Their solution appealed to the court, and the court ordered it. The defendant would be required to wear an ankle monitor that could pinpoint his location 24/7. Besides reporting to Pretrial and providing alcohol and drug spot checks through urinalysis and breathalyzers, Pretrial would require this defendant to wear an ankle monitor. Now everyone would know where he was anytime day or night.

Pretrial Services often boast of this ability to monitor a criminal suspect's release once on bond. Opponents of commercial bail love to mention Pretrial's ability to oversee their defendants. The truth is that Pretrial Services seldom monitor anyone once a suspect is out of custody. The actual companies that do the monitoring are private companies. These private companies contract with Pretrial Services and hold a monopoly on providing those monitoring services for a daily fee. This fee is then paid by the poor, innocent defendant, or at times by tax-paying citizens when the individual released from jail cannot pay. These citizens would include the victims of the same criminal suspects.

In this case, the defendant would not receive his freedom on a bond without first having an electric ankle monitor attached. The tracking device would keep real-time tabs on the

defendant's exact whereabouts. Besides all the other requirements ordered by the court, this criminal suspect would stay in
jail until escorted over to Pretrial, and an electric ankle monitor affixed and turned on.

Once the bail-bonding agent had posted the bond, and Pretrial
had attached the ankle monitor, the criminal suspect was released from jail.

Within twenty-four hours of his release, the criminal suspect
cut off his ankle monitor. Three days later, he left Colorado for
Spokane, Washington.

The criminal suspect who had cut off the monitoring device was
now an official fugitive and had crossed that magical border
called the state line, believing he was home free. This crossing
took place three days after he had cut off his ankle monitor.
For three days, the defendant was allowed time to calmly pack
his bags, clear out his home, and say goodbye to Denver. For
those three days, his cut off ankle monitor laid around with no
purpose.

The private company being paid to monitor the criminal suspect
did not arrive to investigate their ankle bracelet's tampering.
With no reported bail bond violation, the police did not send
out an officer to make an arrest. Neither was the bail-bonding
agent called by Pretrial so that the bail agent could have acted.
Thus, the criminal suspect was afforded a leisurely three days
to pack his bags, disperse, and store his belongings. He had
three days to prepare for his flight from justice. No need to
panic; Pretrial was monitoring him. He had plenty of time.

After learning he was on his way, this criminal suspect's ex-
wife, in fear of her life, contacted the Denver Police, who informed her that his new crime was minor. They would not be
going after him. Since he had crossed the state line, he was out
of their jurisdiction. After crossing the state line, he was not
their problem anymore.

I would note here that Denver Police are some of the finest officers in any force. As it happened, this story is not a criticism of these officers, who seem to daily receive only scorn for their willingness to walk in danger so that others can be free from attack and harm. This story is only about a frightened woman who talked with one law enforcement officer who told her, basically, 'Sorry, you're on your own.'

The Denver District Attorney's Office would not pursue him with an extraditable warrant, as the defendant's charge fell into the non-extraditable category of 'Not important enough.'

In fairness to the Denver District Attorney's office, they cannot pursue every misdemeanor fugitive that runs across the state line. They do not have the funds for this type of pursuit. Their docket has no shortage of criminal suspects whom they are prosecuting. The Denver District Attorney's Office has no downtime. They are always in the mix, attempting to seek justice for victims. However, once a criminal-suspect for domestic violence, charged in Denver, leaves the State of Colorado, the case no longer has viability as an offense for prosecution.

Having received no notification that a dangerous fugitive was headed their way and was a possible threat to the safety of a terrified woman, Spokane law enforcement would not be prepared to act on her behalf, either.

There was only one person who could and would go after this criminal suspect. That was the bail-bonding agent who had posted his bond.

The bail-bonding agent discovered the defendant had cut off his ankle bracelet and fled the state when the suspect failed to meet at a designated time, as required by the bail-bonding agent. When the suspect did not appear, the bail-bonding agent attempted to reach him by phone. He was unsuccessful. At this point, the agent did not file a report with the court. The agent drove out to the suspect's home, which he soon learned was emptied. A block investigation ensued.

Neighbors suggested the defendant was on his way to Texas. The suspect had made many recent references to family and friends in Texas. The neighbors were sure this was his intended destination. They were even able to supply the name of the city where they believed his family lived. The bail-bonding agent found it too convenient that during the three days while packing his bags, the defendant would freely proclaim his destination. *'Hey guys, I'm going to Texas! Please don't tell anyone! Okay?'*

The friends who had initially contacted the bail-bonding agent requesting help in posting the defendant's bond also stated that the criminal suspect had family or knew someone in Texas. However, an individual intent on running is not going to tell his neighbors and friends where he is going. A fugitive may provide hints of where he *is not going* to send the hunters in another direction. But for his real destination, it is his private, hidden agenda that the fugitive does not want others to share. The runner will certainly not tell the cosigners, the individuals who helped free him, where he is going.

The bail-bonding agent's investigation helped him discover a more viable lead that led him in the opposite direction of Texas. The information he obtained led the agent to believe the fugitive had run to Spokane, Washington.

The agent packed his bags and headed northwest. However, having inconsistent witness statements and sketchy details, the first trip turned into a failed operation.

The agent returned to Colorado and intensified his efforts, acquiring intel that pinpointed new areas in the northwest where the fugitive may be hiding. A new plan prepared the agent for a second trip.

The Washington State laws require that a bail-bonding agent from out of state hire a local fugitive recovery agent to assist on any arrest. For this reason, on his second trip, the agent's first project was to visit several bail agencies, all of whom requested extensive contracts for locating and arresting the fugitive.

The bail agencies operating in Spokane should have been able to pinpoint the fugitive's exact location based on the active intel supplied by the bail agent. However, before they even left their office, they wanted a signed contract that ensured them a hefty finder's fee. The agent politely declined and decided to locate the fugitive himself. The Washington statutes requiring a local fugitive recovery agent to assist on any arrest did not preclude the Colorado agent from finding the offender independently.

The agent focused on the area where he believed the defendant to be living and used a grid search, eliminating one neighborhood after another. On the third day, the bail agent found the defendant's jeep parked in a trailer lot east of Spokane. The vehicle, however, was not parked by a specific trailer. The defendant's jeep was left in the general parking area of the lot that housed many trailers. That left the exact location of the fugitive's home in doubt.

The bail agent began a two-day reconnaissance to assess times when the Jeep would appear parked in its own space and when it was gone. The agent needed to narrow the time window in which the defendant might be spotted entering or leaving his vehicle. Contracting with a fugitive recovery agent for the arrest was meaningless until the bail agent had an accurate timeline for the fugitive's arrivals and departures.

The bail agent observed a pit bull chained to a trailer opposite where the jeep was usually parked on the second day. Although the Jeep was not there, the pit bull was a red flag. He matched the description of a dog the criminal suspect was known to own.

On the third day, when the bail agent decided to hit the trailer, a fugitive recovery agent who worked eastern Washington made contact. He had heard the agent was looking for local help and offered his services. The Colorado bail agent accepted.

Meeting a few blocks up from the target trailer park, the two agents agreed on the likely point of access the fugitive would use for entry and then began a long and lengthy surveillance operation.

As the day began to settle into evening, the fugitive's Jeep raced by. The agents waited a few minutes for the Jeep to park and the driver to exit the vehicle. Just because it was the suspect's car didn't mean the suspect was the one driving it.

The fugitive recovery agent assisting the bail agent went to an adjacent lot where he could observe the suspect's trailer through a fence. He confirmed that the suspect had exited his Jeep and was in front of his probable residence.

The bail agent drove into the lot, pulling next to the suspect's vehicle. After completing a visual scan of his target, assuring himself the pit bull was tied and would not present a problem, he exited his car and walked over to a cleanly-shaven man. The fugitive picture was of a man with a full beard. The ID threw the agent for a minute, and so he engaged the man in conversation.

Having downed a few drinks at a local bar, the man with the pit bull was mean-mannered and looking for a fight. He did not like conversing with a stranger asking questions. As the agent continued to talk, he finally asked the individual standing in front of him if he was the criminal suspect wanted in Colorado. At this question, a voice next to the bail agent stated, "That's him!"

The voice belonged to the Washington agent, decked out head to toe like a pinup for a swat gear commercial. He had his Taser drawn and was attempting to fire it when it jammed. The fugitive ran. Along the fence and around the back of the trailer, he sprinted, the Colorado agent taking pursuit.

After passing several trailers, the fugitive tripped over a fence and fell. The bail agent jumped on top of him, hit him with a quick pepper spray shot to the eyes, and it was all over. The fugitive was cuffed and walked back to the scene where he was initially spotted. That was when the police showed up, checked the warrant information, the bail agent's credentials, and allowed for the fugitive's return to Colorado. Before the trip, the bail agent doused his fugitive's face with water, gave him a wet towel, and loaded him up into the transport.

This fugitive was a hardcore actor who had spent his freedom from Colorado in the local Spokane Washington bars, drinking and fighting. He had learned nothing about temper and the ills of violence. However, he had discovered one thing. He'd learned a lesson about commercial bail: when you take off from a commercial bail-bonding agent instead of appearing in court, someone is coming after you. You will not go on the run, leaving behind a broken promise, a broken victim, and a bail-bonding agent who is financially liable for your appearance in court. Someone *is* coming for you.

We *will* come for you.

Bail-bonding agents may not catch every criminal suspect who runs, but for everyone who is apprehended, the warning is clear, and others listen. If you run on a commercial bail, someone is coming for you. When a fugitive is caught and returned to jail, they spread this information to others. That is where the learning occurs: in a jail cell where everyone wants to know what happened. Why were you arrested? Who arrested you? They learn very quickly that if they post a commercial bond and run, the bail-bonding agent will be close behind. This information adds to their bail concept and aids them in making the right decision to appear in court.

And what about the ability of Pretrial Services to monitor defendants to ensure they will appear in court? Their expertise is dependent upon the will of the defendant. Appearing in court will not be based on Pretrial or the private companies that hold monopolies, cashing in on the defendants they are paid to monitor.

Pretrial advocates like to claim they are the experts at Pretrial release and can monitor those out of jail for compliance with bond conditions.

Speaking on their behalf, I would undoubtedly agree with part of their brilliance. They are the experts at releasing criminal suspects. They have no problem opening the cell doors and allowing those arrested as criminal suspects to walk out. They are just not particularly good at putting them back in when they violate their pretrial obligations or fail to appear in court.

The question is, *without the ability to enforce, how is monitoring someone useful?*

Pretrial can list page after page of demands they may place on a defendant. They can force the defendant to wear an ankle monitor, take UA's, and breathalyzers every week. But if they can't enforce the rules they make, what good are their rules?

If police can only watch a bank robber robbing a bank while doing nothing, what is their purpose?

What good are the private companies contracted with Pretrial to monitor criminal suspects when they have no enforcement capabilities? Their ability is limited to collecting the money for each service they provide and filing reports when a criminal suspect fails to follow any of their guidelines. They supply their account to Pretrial Service, which then documents the information and presents it to a court.

When a court, inundated with a flood of new cases, has the time to review the criminal suspect's case, they can hold a hearing. During the hearing, if the defendant appears, the court can determine if they violated their bail bond conditions. If someone shows up for court, the court can order them back to jail.

As a process that allows an individual the freedom of navigation—to avoid imprisonment and run when the urge hits—Pretrial, and the private companies that monitor them, are at the peak of efficiency. While they profit at overseeing what they think they see, they are relatively useless when it comes to guaranteeing a defendant's appearance in court.

The only real power some of these private monitoring companies have is threatening the defendants they monitor if the innocent defendants fail to pay their fees.

Simultaneously, if a criminal suspect on a commercial bail bond violates bail bond conditions, a bail-bonding agent or a fugitive recovery agent has the right of arrest and can and will immediately return the suspect to jail. Once they are again confined, the defendant can appear before the judge and explain the violation. That is accountability. The court can then rule on the viability of the breach. But during the hearing, one thing is assured: the defendant is there in court, not off running the streets.

Monitoring without accountability only serves private companies' profit margins, who have no obligation to take enforcement action once a violation occurs. It would be somewhat like a police department that promises to protect and serve but demands its officers stay at home while forbidding them to patrol the streets. When a crime is committed, a citizen can call a police officer, and the officer can make a report. The officer could then file the report with a court and set everything for a hearing—no need to hit the streets on patrol. The officer can relax at home, watch reruns of *Leave it to Beaver* and answer the phone when a call comes in. Easy breezy! Although electronic monitoring is all the rage, it is a false comfort imposed by private companies that claim it is practical when it often does little more than provide a blanket for Linus.

On May 6, 2016, a thirty-eight-year-old sex offender was arrested for kidnapping two women, who he intended to assault sexually. He accomplished this act while wearing an ankle monitor.

In 2016 in Shelby County, a defendant was found guilty of aggravated robbery and aggravated assault: crimes committed while wearing an ankle bracelet. While attempting to rape one of the women he wanted to kidnap, he even displayed the ankle monitor required to wear from a previous sex case. He thought showing his ankle monitor was a good way to intimidate his victim.

A newspaper report from the *Houston Chronicle* on the growing use of ankle monitors in Texas headlined the following: '***Parolees are shedding ankle monitors for escapes***.' The story talks of the increasing number of parolees snipping off their ankle monitors.

These individuals then commit horrendous crimes. It also revealed details of false alarms and those who commit crimes while wearing the devices.

The fundamental problem with the ankle monitor is that it is only as effective as the individual's willingness to wear it. It may be more valuable for use on a parolee or individual on probation than for a defendant on bond.

As for individuals on bond, without an immediate arrest/compliant force that can act quickly when a monitor rings off, the ankle monitors' promotion far exceeds their actual value. The only thing an ankle monitor does guarantee is that a private company will earn about $300 to $500 per month for every bonded inmate who wears their bracelet.

The only truly effective program is one fashioned after the A21 Program out of Louisiana. Used by bail agents, this system allows a defendant to be monitored 24/7 in real-time. The tracking system, using high-tech ankle bracelets, is attended to by round-the-clock, off-duty firefighters. A bail-bonding agent gets an immediate notification when a defendant tampers with a device or crosses a prohibited geographic barrier.

The bracelets cannot be snipped off with bolt cutters, and when a defendant attempts to remove one, a notification is sent to the bail agent in real-time. The agent then has two options. He can call the individual via a phone embedded in the bracelet or immediately go to the target area and catch the defendant in the act.

This program's strength is the 'Power of Arrest,' a bail-bonding agent has after posting a bond. If an alarm sounds, a bail agent can act immediately and take control of the situation. A report can come later.

If a defendant with a restraining order crosses a red line boundary set by the court in the case of domestic violence, notification is immediate. A defendant approaching the victim's residence or work site can be intercepted in real-time. The bail-bonding agent or the police can then move in, arrest, and take the defendant to jail. The A21 program is a monitoring system with accountability for individuals who can act *now*, not file a report later. On average, they also cost less than other commercial electric monitors currently in use by Pretrial or their assigned business partners.

Although I am not a proponent of ankle monitors on most defendants who are out on bail, if the court orders electronic monitoring, it is the bail-bonding agent who is better suited to track the defendant's whereabouts. A bail agent can then enforce any action that is required. Should the defendant tamper with or otherwise violate any agreement regarding their monitoring, *a bail agent can act in real-time*.

In one California case, an offender, while compliant with probation, was also holding a woman hostage. While on probation/parole, this individual had kidnapped and held prisoner a female who then endured years of sexual violence during her captivity. Throughout these years of slavery, those monitoring the individual had no clue what was going on. They were also clueless of the children the offender fathered through his victim's continual rapes.

The false notion that Pretrial can monitor criminal suspects on a bond is faulty on three fronts:

1. Pretrial seldom monitors anyone. They use private for-profit companies to do their monitoring for them. These private companies have exclusive contracts that assure them of profits but have no responsibility to guarantee anyone that the defendant will appear in court. Neither do they have the Power of Arrest over the defendants they monitor when a violation occurs.

2. Monitoring activities depend on the defendant's honesty. A Pre Trial check-in is only as good as the defendant's willingness to provide accurate information to the agent assigned to their case. During check-in, the defendant will decide on what information he or she gives or omits. Breathalyzers and drug screens can also be fooled and ignored;

   According to one news outlet, a Colorado woman caused a microwave in a 7-11 to explode while attempting to heat her urine before giving a required urine test. Another 7-11 had to put up a sign telling people that using their microwave for heating urine was prohibited. The practice of heating and using pre-selected clean urine had become so common; this 7-11 had to notify customers that heating their urine was forbidden.

Why do criminal suspects being monitored by Pretrial heat up their urine? The urine is not theirs. When a criminal suspect released on bond continues to drink or use drugs, they may need another person's bodily fluid. Cold urine is a giveaway that it is not coming from the person's bladder in front of you. If an individual is required to provide a urine sample, they need to make sure it is warm and toasty. If a clean and sober friend offers their own pee, it must be heated before presenting it as yours.

By heating urine at a 7-11 or similar location, they can make a quick switch at the site requesting the sample before giving their sample. The sample they offer is not theirs, but it is clean and warm.

Regulated monitoring allows for the criminal suspect to counter that monitoring;

3. Pre Trial does not have the power to immediately intercede via an arrest when a criminal suspect violates a bond condition or becomes a threat to others or themselves.

There are also many requirements set that others claim will assure a defendant follow the laws and is not a threat. In one case in Virginia, an individual on a no-bond hold, in jail on rape, strangulation, and abduction charges, had his lawyers argue for his release due to COVD-19. The lawyers claimed this man was in danger of catching COID-19.

The lawyers then presented the Judge with a plan to assure that the defendant's release would not pose a danger to others. The defendant's lawyers explained that he would not be running the streets by requiring the defendant to stay home under house arrest. Everyone would be safe. The Judge agreed and allowed the defendant to post a bond under his attorneys' strict conditions outlined. The defendant would not be allowed to leave his home.

However, on July 29, 2020, police allege that the defendant, Ibrahim E. Bouaichi, did leave his home, returned to Alexandria, and shot and killed his accuser, Miss Dominguez, outside of her apartment.

Miss Dominguez was a native of Venezuela, alone in America. She had no attorneys representing her in court, no one looking out for her.

The problem with monitoring defendants' on a bond is that it has little to no value. Requiring defendants to stay at home is about as effective as the defendant's ability to open the front door. And in the case of Miss Dominguez, Mr. Bouaichi's health appeared to have more value than Miss Dominguez's life.

The only effective monitoring of criminal suspects must be a program that can provide immediate action when needed. That type of control is available when imposed by licensed bail-bonding agents. With their custodial rights over the criminal suspect and their Power of Arrest, they can act while others can only file reports.

No monitoring is 100% effective. Criminals are skilled at finding ways and means of outwitting any monitoring device or system. And without the ability to act immediately, all monitoring is nothing more than a feel-good system of, 'See; we did something!'

And within the truth of Bail Reform, no monitoring is desired. New York recently endowed all criminals suspects with a get-out-of-jail-free card.

How has this worked for New York? Or, should we ask, how has this worked for the criminal suspects? One bank robber was released from jail without bail after his arrest for three bank robberies. With a grateful heart, he then proceeded to rob his fourth bank within hours of his release. However, he can rest easy that there will be no jail cell waiting if the police arrest him again.

This criminal has perfected the art of bank robbery in New York. Go into the bank, give the teller a note demanding all the money, then walk out. If you get arrested, no worries. As long as you don't show a weapon, you are assured a free pass out of jail. The police can detain you, but the jail will not hold you.

Based on New York's bail reform, *Crime-for-Free* program, as long as you do not carry a weapon or use violence, you can rob or steal to your heart's delight. Each time you are arrested, you are freed. It's as simple as that. Go to jail; they are quick to open up the doors to your cell and wish you a good day.

And so as the great fraud of bail reform spreads its dark tentacles across America, it goes from 'We can monitor better" to 'Hey, let's just open the jail doors and let them run free! After all, everyone is innocent!'

Chapter 6: Those Greedy Bail Bondsmen
A *True Story*

His release from prison concluded a three and ½ year sentence.

Usually, an individual sentenced to prison in Colorado knows specific ways to reduce their time behind bars. In most cases, an inmate comes up for a Parole Hearing after serving only 50% of their time. If the Parole Board believes the prisoner has learned his or her lesson and can make it on the streets without committing a new crime, they can allow the prisoner parole; their release from prison subject to specific rules the prisoner must follow.

A prisoner who takes advantage of various prison programs and stays out of trouble can also receive as many as ten days off a month. That means for every 20 days a prisoner serves, they receive a credit of an additional ten days, totaling 30 days for 20. This incentive is to inspire good prison behavior and the involvement of prisoners in rehabilitative measures. The programs offered are designed to help them survive on the streets and turn their lives around.

In the case of our newest fugitive, he did not receive parole or any good time. As he explained it, *'I got no breaks because I was into prison politics.'*

Prison politics did not mean he was running for election as a prisoner representative. It also did not mean he was campaigning for someone else. Prison Politics refers to gang banging while locked up.

Many inmates join and become part of a prison gang in prison for protection, or comradeship, or because it is expected or under threat of harm. These gangs run the cell blocks while dealing with drugs, contraband, and beatings to enforce the rules they decide to set up. Involvement in these gangs often hinders a prisoner's possible early release. In our fugitive case, his gang banging assured him of serving the full sentence handed down by the court.

When he walked out of prison, he had nothing. No one was there for him; no one would help him.

His family would not help him.

His friends would not help him.

His gang affiliations were of no value.

He had no money, and except for what he wore on his back, no clothes, and no place to stay.

Feeling hopeless, he called his old bondsman, or rather bondswoman. She listened to his story and decided to help. That was and is her nature. She believes in touching the lives of others in need.

She provided this man with some clothes, a little money and helped him find a temporary place to live until he could get a job, get on his feet.

Later, after a few months in which this man tried working for a living, he was arrested for domestic violence. He called the bondswoman. She posted a $5,000.00 bond and allowed him to arrange a budget payment because his funds were lacking. She expected him to seek help and get anger counseling while on bail.

After appearing for one or two court hearings, this young man decided he'd had enough of court and Colorado. He determined that going on the run to maintain his freedom was worth more than the kindness that had been provided by the bond-swoman who was there for him when no one else was. He ran to Wisconsin. The Bondswoman contacted an insurance investigator. Could he help? He would try.

The defendant's case involved a domestic violence charge filed as a misdemeanor. For this reason, the court issued the defendant's first warrant as a Colorado State-Wide warrant only. If he left the State of Colorado, Colorado would not extradite him. Once out of the state, he would be home free — his victim, not.

The victim now felt a renewed sense of betrayal. Victimized by a man who told her he loved her yet could not control his anger, she was now also distressed by his departure. Her case would sit as another empty case in a stack of cases that would never go anywhere.

He had hurt her, bailed out of jail, and left the state. He knew well that Colorado would not extradite him on a misdemeanor once he got across that magical state line.

The State of Colorado would not go after him.

Pre-Trial would certainly not track him down.

There was no active police pursuit to find, locate, and return this fugitive.

Politicians were not making TV speeches about the evils of domestic violence while assuring the viewers that this man who had fled from the court's jurisdiction would be hunted down and returned to face justice.

There was only one victim alone and one bondswoman, who had one day shown kindness to an ex-con just out of prison. This bondswoman showed compassion when no one else would.

No one else cared.

This bondswoman called an insurance investigator. He cared. He was angry that after the kindness shown to the criminal suspect, the suspect could turn around and hurt another, then defraud the lady who was there for him after his prison release.

Why did she post the defendant's bond on a domestic violence case? Because he, like all criminal suspects, practice their line before they ever make that bond call. He told the bondswoman how bad he felt and that he was going to seek help. Naturally, he was also innocent of the charges they filed. However, in light of the accusations, he stated he knew it was time to change. Whatever it took, he would change. And he did. He changed into a pair of running shoes and ran. He became a fugitive *On the Run in America.*

There were initially two problems with resolving this case. The first was that the warrant was non-extraditable. In many states, that is irrelevant. Most are glad when a bail bonding agent or fugitive recovery agent shows up to remove a fugitive living in their jurisdiction. These states know that an individual on the run has a higher propensity for violating the law than the average criminal. They do not want their citizens to become prey for these fugitives. And when a state cannot afford the time and cost involved in going after, locating, arresting, and returning these fugitives, due to a cumbersome and costly extradition process, that state's bail bonding agents or fugitive recovery agents can complete the task.

When these agents remove a fugitive from the state to which the offender ran, these agents act as the protector of that state's citizens, who will now not become victims themselves. These agents will prevent another crime and another victim. Their actions will mirror the movie, '*The Minority Report.*' Not because fugitive recovery agents have a sci-fi-computer that projects the next crime to occur at the hands of each fugitive on the run, but because of experience. Escapees who run seldom change anything.

A criminal suspect, escaping from a charge of domestic violence, who has not dealt with his anger, endangers the next woman on his date card. The recovery agent who captures a fugitive escaping jail time on a charge of drunk driving keeps innocent blood off the pavement on the street where that driver might have driven. Preventing a thief from committing fraud, the robber from his or her robbery is often a result of a recovery agent's action. Removing even one fugitive from the streets can stop a crime before it occurs. Protecting an innocent victim and preventing another crime statistic are the benefits of a successful fugitive recovery operation.

Regarding the fugitive who ran to Wisconsin, a second problem overlapped the narrow focus of the warrant issued. Wisconsin does not have commercial bail and does not allow bail agents into their state to capture and return those on the run from the law. Wisconsin has become a form of fugitive haven, aiding and abetting those who flee other states, which are then free to prey on Wisconsin's citizens. It is better to allow the good people of Wisconsin as prey for these fugitives than to allow others to arrest and return them to face justice. Allowing a fugitive's removal by force to serve a sentence is too cruel for Wisconsin politicians. Better their citizens are violated first.

The same politicians will boldly claim that if the state holding the warrant is willing to extradite, then the bail bondsman and fugitive recovery agents are irrelevant. However, this is a deception that darkens the truth. The truth is that states cannot afford to extradite every fugitive who crosses the state line. Even Wisconsin allows many of their own criminals a pass on crime once they leave their state. It's as if the unspoken agreement Wisconsin has made with their defendants is, *'Run Free! We do not want you back. So, Run Free and prosper!'*

How many victims their decisions create, both outside and inside their state, no one will ever know. That is one statistic no one wants to track. No one wants a record of how many criminals victimize innocent individuals while they are on the run. *Because of what the records may reveal, there is no record.*

In overcoming the problematic issues, the investigator requested the bail lady write a motion to the Court. The original warrant needed to be reissued as extraditable. A controversial

move rejected by some judges and county sheriffs, motioning the court was vital to catching the fugitive hiding in Wisconsin.

In the county the fugitive ran from, the court ruled in favor of the motion, reissuing the warrant. The Sheriff's Department then entered the warrant information into the NCIC system (N.C.I.C. The National Crime Information Center.)

Once a defendant's name is entered into NCIC, notification is given to law enforcement officers on the scene, letting them know they have stopped a fugitive wanted by another law enforcement agency in the continental United States. This system also tells the officer if the warrant issued is extraditable. If the state issuing the arrest warrant has not requested extradition, the fugitive walks. As Brad Heath wrote in his USA article, the count of those on the run, walking free on felony warrants without fear of arrest, currently stands at approximately 180,000. These are fugitives with active warrants issued by states that will not extradite them. They are, for all intents and purposes, free to roam the country.

Cost is often the main reason states refuse to insist on the return of their criminals who run across the state line. They do not have the cash or resources it requires to return every fugitive who runs. However, when a state allows commercial bail, it is not the state that will pay the extradition. Those costs are the responsibility of the bail bonding agent.

In the Wisconsin runner's case, the bail bondswoman was fortunate that the judge granted the motion and re-issued the warrant as an extraditable warrant. The Judge believed that Justice was required and thought Justice, without the fugitive return, was not justice at all.

The Sheriff in the county issuing the warrant also desired that the fugitive be caught and returned.

The next problem was the location of the defendant. As Wisconsin law appears to prevent the arrest and removal of a fugitive from their state by a bail bonding agent or fugitive recovery agent, the operation would be delicate. However, with an extraditable warrant, the insurance investigator was determined to locate the defendant. Once found, his arrest and return to Colorado could be arranged.

It was reasonable to assume that Wisconsin would not go all out in locating and returning a Colorado Fugitive wanted for domestic violence. If the defendant were stopped by or bumped into a Wisconsin Police Officer, his arrest was inevitable, but no one would pursue him actively. The question then was, before stopping this fugitive, how much damage could he cause. Who else would suffer first?

With bags packed, the insurance investigator headed for Wisconsin.

Wisconsin is an eye-catching state with rolling hills, minimounts, and artistic landscapes, picture-perfect to the imagination, that draws one into the wonder of the scenery, like an enchanted land.

However, upon arrival, the insurance investigator had little time for enchantment. The agent located a nice motel in Wisconsin, checked in, left his bags, and scouted out the town. It was small and tidy.

The next day the investigator proceeded to the Sheriff's Department with a fugitive packet he had prepared.

Many people who track fugitives enjoy being called Bounty Hunters or Fugitive Recovery Agents. However, this agent practiced his art, the investigation, location, arrest, and culprits return, as an insurance investigator. He investigated insurance fraud in bad bonds and the people who sign those bonds under pretenses. He specialized in tracking criminal suspects released from jail who go on the run rather than go to court.

In Colorado, bail bonding agents are, in fact, licensed insurance agents. Individuals requesting the postings of a bond are signing insurance contracts. They are legally binding insurance agreements. For this reason, when a criminal suspect willingly goes on the run, their act of running becomes a form of insurance fraud. This principle allows the insurance investigator to safeguard the insurance company and bail agent who underwrote the bond.

At the Sheriff's Office, the investigator presented himself and requested to talk with their fugitive task force. He waited in the front as the sheriff's clerk went into the back.

After several minutes, a detective emerged from behind closed doors. He reviewed the agent's papers, extraditable warrant, ID, Bond Forms and discussed the criminal suspect's charges. Then this detective made an excellent suggestion.

'If we have to go out and get this guy, he will sit in our jail for weeks waiting for extradition. If you want to go get him and take him back to Colorado yourself, be our guest."

Because the Colorado investigator had a Power of Arrest over the fugitive, given to him by the bail bonding agent, the agent readily agreed to this offer. Taking the runner back to Colorado would shortcut the extradition process by weeks, maybe even months.

The first goal was locating the fugitive. Another deputy sheriff who learned the investigator was in town helped with this problem. This deputy had contacted the defendant before the Colorado Court reissued the fugitive's warrant as extraditable. She provided the agent with contact information for the defendant and wished him well. How profitable the citizen's safety on the street is when law enforcement willingly works with those, tracking fugitives. Their help and assistance safeguard those whom they promise to serve and to protect. Rather than self-inflated egos interfering in a fugitive's capture or interagency jealousy, a sincere desire to take criminals off the street appeared to be their operational purpose. Their citizens can be proud and thankful for

these men and women who daily face life and death to keep them safe.

In the case of our fugitive, this deputy sharing Intel aided in the quick arrest and removal of this man and the danger he posed to the citizens within their jurisdiction.

The investigator posed as a local insurance investigator trying to resolve a case involving a broken window and rang up the defendant.

'Hi, my name's Mike. I'm an insurance investigator investigating a case of property damage. An elderly couple had their front window smashed. Someone threw a rock and shattered the glass. And while we were questioning neighbors, your name was mentioned.'

'Hey man, I had nothing to do with that,' replied the fugitive.

'I intend to agree,' replied the agent, *'But since your name was mentioned, I need a video statement that you were nowhere around the vicinity where the broken window occurred.'*

The story was created to gain the defendant's trust by bringing up an incident that had never occurred and for which the defendant knew he was not guilty.

'A witness claimed they spotted a man 6' 5," 250 lbs. throw the rock. Your description states you are only 5'9' and no more than 165 pounds. So even though your name came up, I know it could not have been you. However, I need to clear you off as a potential suspect candidate. A video statement will show it couldn't be you. Is that cool? I'll even buy you a beer while we talk.'

Although hesitant, the defendant knew he had thrown no rock at any window and so felt safe enough to arrange a meet the following evening at the local bar.

Arriving early, the agent parked in the street at the rear of the bar. He had already removed his Colorado license plates upon entering the small town. The plate removal would help avoid any possibility of a chance sighting by the fugitive. It is often the little things that can give a hunt away.

In the bar, the agent set up his video and busied himself with a game of pool. After a short wait, the criminal suspect walked in with a larger man as his escort. The big man was his protection, his own insurance policy. They walked up to the bar and ordered a drink.

The agent watched until the man accompanying the fugitive left his side for the jute box. The agent made his move and walked up to the culprit with an outstretched hand.

'Hey, I think you're here to meet with me, right?'

The fugitive did not hesitate and offered his hand. *'Yea.'* In that instant, the agent shook his right-hand, slapping on a cuff with his left.

'You're under arrest.'

'Hey! You lied to me!' yelled the fugitive. *'You said we would just talk.'* A struggle began. The investigator quickly cuffed the defendant to himself to prevent the offender from squirming free and running off.

As the struggle moved away from the bar and toward a pool table, the fugitive's big friend quickly took notice. He approached as if to help.

For a brief moment, the arrest was touch and go. However, simple verbal threats and a quick assurance blended nicely to keep the fugitive's friend from any physical interference.

'Stay away,' the agent warned the friend. *'If you interfere, you will go to jail for obstruction of justice! Your friend has a warrant for property damage. The bond is only $300.00. After I take him to jail, you can quickly bond him out. But if you interfere, you'll both go to jail, and no one will get out!'*

The ruse worked well enough on the friend, as the agent grappled with the fugitive pushing him up against a pool table. He repeated the warning directly to the defendant.

'Look, you keep fighting me; I will book you in jail on multiple felonies! Right now, you have a simple $300.00 misdemeanor warrant. Cooperate, and you'll be in and out of jail in no more than 30 minutes. You'll be back at the bar in no time. But if you continue to fight, I'll file so many charges that you will never get out.'

This conversation took place in firm whispered threats while the investigator jammed the fugitive up against the pool table.

The fugitive relented, and the agent was able to turn him around and cuff both hands behind his back.

As the agent began to walk the fugitive out of the back door, his friend began to follow. The agent cautioned the friend.

'Sir, you need to stay back. As soon as I book your friend into the jail right behind the bar, I'll contact you, and you can post his new bond. Good?'

'Okay,' said the fugitive's friend. The agent walked the defendant out of the back door and over to his waiting car.

'I am required to drive you into the jail through the Sallyport,' the agent stated as he positioned the fugitive in the back of the vehicle. Once in the car, the agent shackled the fugitive's feet.

'Sorry, but this is just the protocol."

With the fugitive secured, the agent got into the driver's side and pulled out.

After a few blocks, when it was apparent, the investigator was driving away from the local county jail, located immediately behind the bar, the fugitive asked what was going on.

'You're going back to Colorado,' stated the agent bluntly. *'I have a warrant for your arrest for jumping bond in Colorado, and that's where I'm delivering you.'*

'There isn't a $300.00 bond,' asked the fugitive.

'No,' answered the agent.

The fugitive was stunned. However, after the truth of the situation set in, the criminal suspect could do nothing more than slump back into his seat. And he cried.

Arresting anyone is not always an easy thing to do. To come upon a fugitive and immediately take away their freedom by placing them in custody can feel cruel.

His arrest was the very last thing this fugitive expected on this day. He was first shocked and then collapsed into hopelessness. His life, to him, had just ended.

However, nothing had ended, and this man's life was just beginning. A fugitive on the run has no beginning, only a continuation of a criminal past. A man or woman fleeing justice will seldom change behavioral patterns while evading an arrest. It is just after catching a fugitive, stopping them in their tracks, that an opportunity to review his or her life is provided.

A captured criminal suspect can decide that their torn and ruined life must now be surrendered. Within the pause of their confinement, they may find the will to change those things wrong. They can choose a new life away from madness, hatred, uncontrolled anger, and their criminal life of destruction. Their arrest stops the clock and offers them the moment of reflection they had no time for on the streets. They may not change or alter anything, but at least they have the moment immediately after their arrest to think about it.

After an arrest, a fugitive can contemplate their life and choose a different path going forward.

Many a fugitive say that their first feeling after being arrested is a feeling of relief. These captured runners have comfort that the unseen tension and constant need to look over their shoulders are at an end.

Although this was not the first feeling the fugitive in our story had, he would soon come to understand that he needed to resolve his past before he could begin a new future.

On the trip back to Colorado, the fugitive did begin to realize the issues that had so far damaged his life and hurt others. He seemed determined to start anew. Only time would tell.

He was returned to the jail in the county in Colorado from which he had run. The system worked as it should. However, it worked because Colorado has Commercial Bail. It worked because a Judge was willing to issue the extraditable warrant. This accomplishment succeeded because one Sheriff cared about one victim.

'I am here to serve and protect you, each of you, even the lone victim who was abused by a criminal-suspect, who fled the state. I am here for you too.' And he was. The actions of both the sheriff and the court were enough to initiate one violent fugitive return on the run in America.

While being escorted to the jail, even the suspect-criminal stated he had a strange feeling of calmness about him. Maybe this would be his new beginning. Perhaps this suspect-criminal could now get a grip on his temper and have a better life than he had before, with deeper relationships void of violence.

Fugitives on the run seldom change. Unless they change or are taught to change, others will continue to suffer. Arresting a criminal gives them a new opportunity to improve, to start anew. On the run, there is only the illusion of beginning again. Once captured, the actual process of change can begin. Returning a fugitive to the hands of justice affords that beginning.

And the Victim? She got to see that justice works. She got to hear about a Wisconsin detective who had a heart for the victim and wanted to protect other women in his state from the same fate. She was able to watch how a Court, a Sheriff's Department, and an insurance investigator all worked together to return the criminal suspect who hurt her. This victim got to experience the Justice System's success that believes a victim is worth the effort. She **was** worth the effort, and everyone's actions showed her she was.

It is unfortunate that in the mad rush for bail reform, a reform that frees prisoners without accountability, the victim is omitted from the equation. There is no mention of the word '**Victim**' in bail reform, only the hundreds of innocent criminal suspects in jail because they are poor. They are not guilty of domestic violence, drinking, and driving, theft or burglary, robbery, sexual assault, or any other myriad crimes against persons. No one is guilty, and there are no more victims. **How can there be any victims when everyone in jail is innocent?**

The bail bondswoman never showed any animosity toward the suspect-criminal, even after he decided his freedom was more important than doing what was honorable. Also, though she had been the only one to help this man when his own family refused him, it was not enough for him to do what was right. What was enough? An insurance investigator traveling to Wisconsin, locating, arresting, and returning with the fugitive was enough. This bondswoman blended compassion with accountability. The two are not exclusive of each other.

If this criminal suspect's bond had been through a government-run Pre-Trial program, the fugitive would still be in Wisconsin. He might be luring another woman into the arms of his unchecked anger and madness. Another innocent woman would be at risk from his volatile temper, a volcano simmering, ready to explode.

The Critics of bail bonding like to spout out clichés they hope will cast a dark shadow across the bail bonding profession. These sound bites are used repeatedly as truths but have little to do with reality.

A favorite of bail opponents is, ***Bail Bonding Agents are greedy! They are merely trying to protect a multibillion-dollar industry!***

I have never met a billionaire bail bondsman! For the most part, Bail bonding agents are just individuals earning a middle-class salary, striving to support their families. In Colorado, the average yearly income for a bail bondsman can range from $40,000 to $80,000. Bail Bonding Agents want to pay the rent, put food on the table, buy clothes for their children. They want money on hand when a medical emergency arises. They want to pay their bills.

They want to earn a workable living.

If earning a workable living to support one's family is greedy, then perhaps every working man and working woman in America are guilty of never-ending greed!

Claiming bail is a billion-dollar industry is like saying the independent farmers of America are greedy, in a multibillion-dollar industry where they force us to pay for food, or else we starve! By combining all farmers into one category, one can inflate the money earned by these same farmers. These false sound bites allow others the appearance of being billionaires. However, they are not. They work hard and deserve to make a living.

Bail Bonding agents each act as an independent agent, operating their own business. They receive no paid health insurance, no vacation time. They do not receive lucrative retirement accounts. They earn what they earn, week by week.

In Colorado, many bail bonding agents are females, and single mothers, trying to provide for their child or children as best they can. These are women who dare to enter a sometimes-dangerous profession to earn a decent wage and support their families. And they are good at it. However, they are not rich. And they are not greedy. They are hard-working and determined.

The same is true for their male counterparts, who also choose this profession to support their family and ensure justice with accountability.

Bail bonding is an equal-opportunity business, open to Females and Males, Blacks, Whites, Hispanics, Asians, or anyone else who decides to step into this risky yet honorable profession.

Most bail bonding agents in Colorado earn a middle-class income with no guarantees. They have no safety nets and live and work from week to week, like other workers across America. Although critics of bail would have you believe every bail bonding agent is a greedy over-weight, cigar-smoking billionaire, this image is ludicrous. It is merely the image they wish to paint those they do not care for, so others will also not care for them. When people are unable to have an honest debate, they revert to name-calling. Sound bites are quickly spoken, and oft-repeated words can have the power to convince through rep-etition, even when untrue.

As in the case of the Wisconsin fugitive, being released from prison, with no one there to help, it was a bail bondswoman that offered to take care of his needs. And most bail bonding agents have this same standard of care. They each reach out and touch their communities in a meaningful and beneficial way.

In each of the communities where they reside, bail bonding agents are practitioners in the art of caring and giving. They support a wide range of charities. In Chaffee County, Colorado, a single mother supporting her child through bail commits 10% of her monies to a victim's fund.

In Eagle County, Eagle Bail supports Vail's Shop with a Cop on Christ-mas, where disadvantaged young children with no money can enjoy the season of lights. After collecting donations for the year, a volunteer police officer accompanies each child on a Christmas shopping spree to buy gifts for the child's family. The program brings together law enforcement and the underprivileged in the light of hope.

Another bail bonding agent helps support the disadvantaged through donations.

From the homeless to the needs of those they serve, bail bonding agents are there, quietly reaching out to touch another life with hope. These are not Photo-Ops, for public consumption, but people, affecting others' lives in quiet moments when no one is watching. They do not act out for the TV, but for the cause, because it is in their hearts to act this way.

Because they live and deal with the hurt and marginalized, bail bonding agents often help those who cannot help themselves. Their actions are not for self-glory, but so others can feel the hand of hope.

Critics love faulting bail bonding agents for making a living at another's expense, but so does everyone who works within the justice system. The Justice System is not one sizeable non-profit organization filled with non-paid volunteers.

Individuals working in government-run Pre-Trial programs not only make a decent weekly salary but enjoy health benefits, an attractive retirement package, and bear no responsibility if the defendant they release fails to appear in court.

Attorneys defending criminal suspects require retainers that can reach into the thousands before they even walk into a courtroom to represent a defendant.

Judges often earn six-figure salaries. Court clerks receive wages and benefits to help them care for their needs and families.

All these individuals make a living in the justice system.

Many private companies also earn profits in the justice system. Their earnings start before the individual arrested is even released from jail.

Private phone companies now run many jail phone services. Inmates or their families can be required to pay up to $15.00 for a simple 5-minute phone call. In the tens of thousands of dollars, the profits from these calls are then split up between the county jail holding the defendants and the private company running the operation. These jailed, innocent individuals must pay exorbitant fees to make one phone call and try to explain to their family in five minutes why they are locked up. One brief phone call per day can run a family up to $450.00 per month.

Once out of jail on a government-run pretrial release, these same poor innocent individuals can be required to pay a monthly fee to pre-trial for supervision. Freed poor people are then expected to pay private companies from $100.00 to $450.00 each month for random UAs (Urinalysis Tests), blood tests, and ankle monitors or *any* other costs that are determined will maintain control. The fees charged by these private companies for monitoring individuals on a bond are paid by the indigent innocent criminal suspects caught in the monitoring companies 'net of profitability.' These defendants become mini ATMs to support the private companies that enjoy monopolies and have exclusive contracts with government pre-trial agencies utilizing their services — a guaranteed profit margin with no accountability.

These private companies do not need to advertise. Pre-Trial provides the company's clients free of charge. And if their clients fail to pay for any service required? Back to jail, they go. It is a safeguarded monopoly of profit whose success is guaranteed by Pre-Trial. It may be interesting to know who exactly has a financial interest in each of these government-guaranteed, private monopolies.

All these individuals, whether working in the justice system as government employees, pre-trial agents, attorneys, judges, and the private companies that serve Pre-Trial, all enjoy guaranteed wages, health benefits, retirement accounts, and profits. However, no one is accountable if a defendant fails to appear in court. Not one of these individuals will lose a dollar, a night's sleep, or any other benefit because a defendant they released on bond and supposedly supervised fails to appear for a court hearing.

When a bail bond agent posts a bond, he or she is immediately accountable for the defendant. If a bail bonding agent posts a $1,000.00 bond for a defendant, who fails to appear in court, the bail bonding agent is responsible to either locate, arrest, and return the defendant to jail or pay the $1,000.00 bond. If a bail bonding agent fails to find, arrest, and return the defendant to prison and pays the $1,000.00 bond, they will then need to post ten other $1,000.00 bonds to break even. They have no automatic health-care plan or a retirement package.

A first-time D.U.I. Case in Colorado usually has a bond amount of $1,000.00. A bonding agent will charge $150.00 to post the bond and be responsible for assuring the defendant appears in court. Out of this money, the bail bondsman will pay insurance fees, taxes, and costs. And, as already stated, the defendant's failure to appear could cost the agent $1,000.00.

Attorneys representing the first time D.U.I. offenders earn between $2,000.00 and $5,000.00 or more per case. First-time D.U.I. Offenders found guilty will, by state statute, all receive the same sentence. It does not matter if they hire a private attorney whose rates can range from $2,000.00 to $5,000.00, or if they represent themselves. If they are found guilty, they all face the same sentence. Unless there are mitigating circumstances, an attorney representing a defendant in a DUI case may be nothing more than a glorified babysitter.

Where is the greed?

The point here is not that Judges and Private Attorneys do not deserve their salaries or earnings. They have an essential part to play in the justice system. We are not even claiming that others who earn a living in the system should not. We are merely sharing the facts. And when the facts are known, the truth is that bail bonding agents earn a living, and that is all they receive. They take risks and go after those who attempt to evade the justice system designed to keep everyone safe. Bail Agents chase down the fugitive on the streets, and often, as stated, again and again, a bail agent can be a victim's last hope for justice.

In truth, commercial bail bonding is, for the most part, run by small independent bail bonding agents. These agents are each involved in their communities and take their jobs seriously. And when the success of a bail bonding company allows it to grow, typically, so does their effectiveness in reaching out to go after those who go on the run. One major bail bonding company in Colorado, Mary Ellen's Bail, once tracked a fugitive to Viet Nam. This fugitive was then arrested and brought back to face justice, all on Mary Ellen's dime. These actions highlight commercial Bail's value.

The only billionaires I have ever known or heard of (never met but heard of) involved in the bail bonding industry are John and Linda Arnold, of the Arnold Foundation. The Arnold Foundation is the organization that promotes its assessment tool as the answer to bail reform. The same assessment tool the Governor of New Mexico found misleading and disastrous, endangering her citizens.

John Arnold is also the same man who walked away from Enron with an 8-million-dollar bonus in his pockets as Enron's workers and retirees, who had spent a lifetime working for Enron, lost their jobs and pensions in the company's bankruptcy filing.

In a moment, in a court ruling, Enron's workers lost everything Enron had promised them. One day, they had pensions, pensions they had worked for, for years, looking forward to retirement. The next day, Enron persuaded a court to nullify their pensions, and they ended up with nothing.

In fact, during the period that John Arnold made over 600 million for Enron, Enron stock tumbled. While the shares fell, the pensioners were not allowed to sell the Enron stock they had invested in over the years to secure their futures. By preventing them from selling their stock, their futures became nothing more than lost hope.

In Oregon, workers of an Oregon Utility Company taken over by Enron lost hundreds of thousands of dollars.

Employees not only lost their retirement but lost their jobs, their health benefits, and their entire life savings.

In one year, from 2000 to 2001, Enron stock dropped from around 91 dollars a share to nothing. During this same period, Jon Arnold made Enron 600 million dollars and walked away at the end of 2001 with a cool 8 million.

Mr. Arnold's cool eight million bonus was a stark contrast to the losses a man named Mr. Maddox endured. A 30-year employee of Enron, who had his entire savings invested in Enron stock, a total of around $1.3 million, Mr. Maddox ended up with nothing. He never saw the crash coming. Over 30 years working for Enron, Mr. Maddox was led to believe in Enron and, encouraged by Enron, invested in their stock.

How is it Mr. Maddox, a plant manager, working for Enron faithfully for 30 years, can end up losing everything he owned, and yet John Arnold gets to walk away with an 8-million-dollar bonus? Perhaps because John Arnold was not a plant manager, but a trader for Enron, betting on the rise and fall of energy stocks, the same stocks that an investigation showed were repeatedly manipulated by Enron.

Mr. Maddox now, as of 2012, is forced to spend his golden years mowing pastures to earn enough money to rent a run-down East Texas farmhouse.

As Mr. Arnold attempts to bulldoze over the bail bonding industry with a computer-driven questionnaire by offering the government grant money, perhaps he can spare a grant for Mr. Maddox. Why doesn't Mr. Arnold also set up grants for all the Enron workers who lost everything? Possibly, John Arnold would be kind enough to open the door to his mansion and allow Mr. McDonald to use a spare bedroom.

However, just as bail reform never mentions the victims, neither did Enron account for the employees who all suffered. After all, they were only victims as well.

Whether through ignorance, naivete, or intentional hatred of others, those pushing bail reform ought to heed to the cares of those who will suffer from their push, rather than the criminals who will profit from it. Their cries of, **_Those Greedy Bail Agents'_** are nothing more than political sound bites, used to dress their cause in righteousness. However, if one looks closely, their purpose is only clothed in the lawlessness of those who joy in their new revolving door justice. In and out, no cares or responsibilities, because the only victims are arrested for cheating, stealing, or robbing others.

Chapter 7: Freedom is JUST One Arrest Away
A True Story

Walking through the casino, the insurance investigator kept his eyes open for the Bonnie and Clyde couple from Texas. Although they had yet to kill anyone, their fraud, theft, cheating, and stealing would endear them to the criminal world of drugs and those on the run in America.

Besides breaking into the mother's safe and making off with Mom's retirement savings secured in the collection of valuable coins, the couple had also cleared out mommy's guns. Now their pockets, wallet, and purse were loaded with cash. Their weapons were loaded with ammo. They were fired up and ready to play, out on the town at their favorite spot: Central City, Colorado, for another all-night gambling spree.

When he first received the case, the insurance investigator began his investigation by charting out various locations visited by the fearless duo. A map with a detailed timeline showcased the Central Point of their destined desire.

When they fled from Texas to avoid court, they had jumped commercial bonds for fraud, leaving two bail agents with $25,000 in losses. Their journey to Colorado was dressed up in the façade of her mother's illness, who was currently in the hospital. Not a daughter to ignore a sick mom, the female fugitive took her boyfriend, and together they traveled west.

Their adventure led them to Colorado and her mother's home, where the welcome mat had been laid out. They moved in, spilling over with concern for Mom and her care.

They also appeared to have a keen sense of concern regarding Mom's valuables. Roaming around mom's garage while she lay in the hospital, they came upon a safe, promising new adventure. They broke open the safe and realized that the coin collection, worth thousands, and the guns inside could offer a spark of life into their somewhat lost existence.

So, while Mom healed at the local hospital, these two lovebirds emptied her safe and headed to their favorite hot spot for a weekend of drugs and gambling. The couple left their cares and their mother behind to enjoy the life of high rollers in Central City.

Although the insurance investigator had determined that Central City was the couples' primary choice, the exact casino was uncertain. A pattern showed the most probable days, nights, and times the lovers' team might appear at any given spot. However, any impulse, win, or loss could take these two in another direction.

Arriving after a day of calculating guesswork, the agent parked and began a walk-through of each casino. It was still early, and he'd learned that the criminal twosome typically hit the casino floors around 2 to 3 am. The agent began showing their picture to the floor security personnel to see if anyone had spotted either suspect. Knowing which casino they might make their appearance in would help the agent prepare the arrest.

While visiting one casino, security informed the agent that they preferred the agent to make any arrest attempt with police presence. The agent then contacted the local police and set up a meet.

The agent delivered two fugitive packets and provided his Intel to the officer at the station. The officer ran both names for warrants, and two popped up. However, only one was extraditable: if found, the police would take the female into custody, and the investigator would take the other. After allowing the officer to make copies of all papers, the agent left.

A couple of hours later, the agent received a call from the local police. They believed they had the suspect's location. They asked if the agent wanted to meet them at the suspect hotel. The agent did.

At the hotel, the police disclosed the fugitives' room number. They also confirmed that based on hotel security cameras, both suspects were in their room.

The police had a plan of operation they believed would draw the duo out into the open. Officers had the front-desk call to say there was a problem. A card the loving pair used to book the room appeared faulty. Could they come to the front desk and sort it out? The investigator cringed.

If he were a fugitive staying in a hotel with drugs, active warrants, and a lot of stolen cash, he would not be so trusting. A front hotel desk ringing and claiming there were problems would cause alarm bells to chime. He would never go down to the hotel desk but would quickly rush out the back door. However, this was not his turf, and other players were in command.

As the front desk called the suspect room, the police officers hid on either side of the lobby just out of sight of anyone that might be entering. If either fugitive entered the lobby, they would pounce.

The agent sat on a bench facing the elevator. He scanned each face if either fugitive tried to exit rather than enter the area targeted for their arrest.

The minutes dragged on, the tension rose, but no one answering to the fugitive's names entered the hotel lobby. The investigator was restless. The front desk called the room again. *"Please, could you guys spare a couple of minutes to get this card problem resolved, please?"* The suspects replied that they would, but neither left their room.

After a bit more time elapsed, an officer approached the agent. *"So, look, we are going to go up to the room and knock on the door."*

"What if they don't answer?" The agent could only imagine the panic that could take hold if one of the fugitives looked out the peephole of their hotel room and spied police officers standing there.

The police officer replied, *"If they don't answer, we can always come back tomorrow."*

Come back tomorrow? Are you kidding me? Knock on their door today and come back tomorrow, and no one will be in that room.

"Why don't you let me knock on the door?" the investigator prodded. *"Or better yet, I can go to the hotel front desk and get a passkey. Then I'll go into the room and bring these two out."*

The officer felt uncomfortable with this approach and stammered a bit before declining the offer.

"Can I go up with you?" asked the investigator.

"Okay," said the officer. *"But we only have the authority to arrest the female. The male's warrant is not extraditable, so we cannot help you with him. You will have to arrest him on your own."*

Riding the elevator up, one of the police officers whispered to the lead officer, *"Why don't we let him knock first."*

The investigator crossed his fingers. *'Please, please say yes.'*

On the target floor, the group proceeded down the hall to the fugitive's room. The officer in charge then relented and allowed the investigator to take front and center. The police officers hid out of sight on either side of the door.

The investigator knocked on the door, then looked off down the hall as if bored. If either fugitive looked through the peephole, he did not want to seem too interested. He knocked again.

Finally, he heard the door's bolt unlocking, and the door opened a crack. The investigator ignored polite niceties, using his shoulders to slam open the door. He then shoved the stunned male fugitive up against a wall, cuffing him behind his back. *"You're under arrest,"* he stated as he moved the suspect further into the room, in front of him as a barrier, till he was able to set eyes on the girlfriend.

Meanwhile, in the hallway, the officers, not wanting to violate any laws but in a state of mild excitement, hollered, *"May we come in?"*

"Yes, you may," replied the investigator.

The girlfriend stood by a bed in a state of shock. As the police entered, they explained to the girl that they had an extraditable warrant out of Texas for her arrest.

The investigator shared the same arrest info from a Texas warrant with the boyfriend. However, the agent stated that he was going to transport the boyfriend back to Texas himself. The boyfriend requested a set of keys. As the agent looked for the keys, opening a couple of bags on the bed, he came across a couple of thick wads of hundreds. At least several thousand dollars in hundreds stuffed in money bags.

After arresting the girlfriend and searching the room, the police found the couple's drug stash.

As the agent tried to maneuver his prisoner out of the door, the fugitive spoke to his other half. *"Hey, do you remember the $5,000 we saved and set aside to pay off our van? Where did you put it?"*

The girlfriend didn't answer, and the agent pushed his prisoner out of the room. The thought that his suspect and sweetheart had saved $5,000 to pay off a van or any other bill was ridiculous. At the time, it was believed that the money had been earned from dealing drugs. Only later was it evident that they had gotten the cash by breaking into the girlfriend's mother's safe while the mother was at the hospital. They had stolen thousands of dollars' worth of coins that Mom had saved over the years for retirement or an emergency.

The agent knew his fugitive's real desire was to have a stash of money for his trip back to Texas. If he had cash on him, he could bail out of jail upon his arrival.

The police questioned the investigators' prisoner concerning the drugs, but he denied any illegal substance responsibility. Of course, he wouldn't know a thing about drugs sitting atop a dresser in their room. The maid probably left it there, hoping for a nice tip!

After questioning his prisoner, the police allowed the investigator to remove his capture from the area. The fugitive was escorted down the hall, hands clasped behind his back, and into the elevator. On the main floor, passing slot machines, card tables, and the glaring stares of onlookers, the fugitive's thoughts were his own, as he proceeded on in silence. He was maneuvered through the crowds and out the door. In the transport vehicle, secured and shackled, the prisoner took a deep breath. His run was over.

Fortunately, the stolen weapons were not in the room when the suspects were taken into custody. With a gun in hand, it is often easier to pull a trigger than to surrender. In the blink of an eye, a nonviolent criminal becomes one of violence. The arrest that ends peacefully today is only a prelude to the dangers waiting in tomorrow. That was the reason for the door being slammed open. Speed and quickness of action can often end a violent standoff before it occurs.

The trip to Texas was uneventful. The fugitive was cuffed and shackled in the back seat, fast asleep while the investigator drove. Criminal suspects who live in the haze of drugs, awake for days, never see the end. After their arrest, with no more drugs are available, they fall out to the world.

The agent planned to cross the state line into Texas and surrender the defendant at the first jail he found. Although the defendant's warrant was not an extraditable state-to-state warrant, it was a statewide warrant for any police officer in Texas. Any Texas jail should have taken custody of the fugitive.

Once in Texas, after locating the first county jail, the agent drove to the front doors and rang the buzzer.

Can I help you?" came a voice from the other side of the intercom.

"*Yes, Sir,*" answered the agent, who then gave his name, explaining that he had a fugitive in his vehicle. Would the jail take him? "*I understand that transporting a fugitive across the state of Texas has certain requirements that I might not meet and so thought surrendering him right away was the best option. His warrant is a state-wide warrant out of Texas.*"

The intercom voice was silent a moment before replying, "*Well, you may have already violated the law by bringing him across the state line.*"

And once again, we observe a state's earnest desire to protect fugitives. That some jurisdictions refuse to extradite their criminals once they cross a state line is understood. These states do not want to bear the cost of such extraditions. However, here, they considered the return of one of their very own fugitives a possible crime. At times, the insanities of law enforcement and statutes enacted by state legislatures that ensure felons' rights are beyond understanding. No wonder criminal suspects go on the run. They know only too well that no one wants them back.

The guard on the intercom left to call the local judge. The investigator waited in the dark. The fugitive slept.

When the guard returned, his answer was firm. "*Sorry, we will not accept him.*"

The investigator shook his head. In Texas, laws for transporting prisoners dictate specific outlines that must be followed. This fugitive had been arrested legally in Colorado, was the

investigators' prisoner, and had active warrants out of Texas for fraud. However, this sheriff's department refused to accept the prisoner.

Many states use private companies that specialize in transporting criminal suspects from one jail to another or across state lines. These professionals are approved and relied on as legally viable transport operations. However, it would require another book to document and tell the tales of criminals who have escaped while being transported in these cross-country vans. Stories would include van drivers who were tied up, beaten, and left on the side of the road while their van scooted on down the highway.

Furthermore, inmates transported via the van system endure days with long hours of being cuffed and shackled while riding from one jail to another. Inmates have been told to use their pants when needing to take a leak if the van driver does not feel like stopping. The prisoners eat the minimal offerings supplied by the van drivers. A defendant can also be a few miles from their destination when the van driver receives a call to detour for another pickup. These altered road plans add days to an already long trip.

I have never lost a fugitive in my professional life of arresting and transporting criminals from state to state. No one has ever escaped. Individuals within my custody are taken care of, fed well, and allowed frequent stops to stretch their legs, get a breath of air or use the restrooms when they need to and as often as they need to.

It is unfortunate that legislatures who have no clue regarding what bail-bonding agents do and how they do it think they themselves are the specialists in some states.

In our Texas fugitive case, the insurance investigator decided he would take the prisoner to the county where the charge originated. This fugitive was very appreciative that he would not be riding in a prison van in an orange suit. He did not wish to be treated like an animal or a freak at a sideshow.

After his surrender to a Texas jail where his charge originated, and after the agent returned to Colorado, the female fugitive's mother called. She thanked him for having both her daughter and the boyfriend arrested. She was crushed that her own daughter, and her daughter's boyfriend, whom she had made feel welcome in her home, had broken into her safe and stolen her collector coins. Those coins were saved for her retirement or an emergency. She also explained that the criminal couple had taken guns she had kept in the safe.

The investigator called one of the police officers that assisted in the couple's arrest, explaining the break-in of the mother's safe. He supplied the mother's contact info and gave the name of the detective investigating the safe's robbery.

Meanwhile, in Texas, a court released the returned fugitive. The court thought it right to reinstate the fugitive's bond and give him another chance. Sure, if the culprit could not get away the first time, maybe his second try would be more fruitful.

Out of jail, the boyfriend once again fled Texas. He returned to Colorado, retrieved his van, which held the stolen guns and lots more cash, posted a bond for his girlfriend's Texas warrant, and off they went. There was no need for the boyfriend to post a bond for his girlfriend's Colorado drug charges: she received a Pretrial *Crime-for-Free* bond on that case. Of course, she *did* promise to return for court.

Before her return court date, another insurance investigator on the case of mom's stolen coins called the arresting agent to obtain any details relevant to the next hearing. At the hearing, he hoped he could convince the judge to take this female back into custody. However, on the day of the trial, one person was missing. Who was it? And after she had promised, she would appear! Who could have known, right?

Where is this duo of crime today? Hopefully, they have fled to one of the states that cherish and care for the rights of a fugitive. Maybe they will go to New York. If they only cheat and defraud others, they will never have to spend a night in jail or a day in court: night and day just to play!

Bail reform is not reform; it is merely the release of criminal suspects without accountability or care.

Chapter 8: Establishing truth In Bail Reform

For truth in bail reform, accountability and victim care must always be at the center.

Trying to claim bail-bonding agents are evil is not the truth. Are there corrupt bail-bonding agents? What is one profession free of corruption?

Every occupation has its bad players, police, and judges to mechanics and even daycare workers. There are unethical private attorneys. There are also plenty of corrupt politicians who have been caught stuffing their pockets with our people's cash. Yes, every occupation has its share of those who cheat, deceive, and hurt others. However, we do not abolish the profession; we prosecute the individual who crossed the line.

The strength of the justice system is found within the courts that uphold that system. If no one appears for court, there can be no justice system. Without courts, there is only chaos and vigilante groups meeting justice according to their own inflated feelings of self-righteousness or resentment and anger. We see where this vigilante justice leads when we watch the beating of a man who was attacked by Portland rioters. Even as this innocent man tried to avoid those who ran after his truck, not wanting him to escape, after his vehicle crashed, they dragged him out of his truck, into the street, and beat him mercilessly. He had nothing to do with George Floyd. He was just someone in a truck trying to bypass the violent criminal rioters.

On the east coast, it is naive to believe that New York career criminals are not re-evaluating their own techniques. If they can rob, cheat, and steal without fear of jail, their freedom is assured. New York's policy is the height of insanity. It is not bail reform; it is the surrender of Gotham City to the Joker.

The concept that everyone in jail is a poor innocent person is a lie.

The entire bail reform process is part of the criminalization of America. As the movement flies across the country, degrading police, ignoring victims while promoting the criminal on the street corner, injustice reigns. And now, as New York has decided that criminals should not be locked up, we have crossed the stage of lawful to the darkness of lawlessness. One can only wonder why this push for disorder persists. What is the real agenda?

For the most part, violent criminals did not begin their lifestyles with gun robberies, stabbing, kidnappings, and other assorted menacing acts. They started as thieves, cons, and small-time hustlers. Perhaps New York believes that if they show these crooks mercy via *Crime-for-Free* releases, these offenders will display their gratitude by not going violent. These non-violent crooks of today will maintain their kind and considerate thievery. Their ongoing cheating and note-passing bank robberies will be a low-profile form of appreciation to New York for not locking them up.

Bail agents know their business is not one of thanks. Everyone is glad when a bail-bonding agent is there to help. However, when a defendant fails to appear in court, and the chase is on, bail-bonding agents and fugitive recovery agents become the targets. It is always their fault. Yet each day, hundreds of fugitives are arrested across the country by bail agents and bail enforcement. These arrests are, for the most part, conducted quietly, quickly, and without harm. Back in jail, the individual has pause to review and possibly change their lives. Every day, bail-bonding agents and fugitive recovery agents face the danger of the streets, taking on those who do not want to obey the law and those who refuse to appear in court.

Furthermore, many times, commercial bail is a victim's last hope for justice. For each time a bail agent or fugitive recovery agent takes one runner off the streets, a victim is assured that justice can now move forward. When bail agents capture a fugitive, one crime will not take place. A family on an evening outing will not have their lives crushed by an intoxicated driver. The drunk on the run from the state next store will not broadside them.

Sally's date will not end in a bloody scene of uncontrolled rage. Her partner will not be the one running from another jurisdiction, avoiding court on a domestic violence charge: before their date, a fugitive recovery agent captured him.

The worker at the local 7-11 will not face the fugitive holding a knife, demanding his money. A bail agent took him into custody earlier that morning.

Police will not find a young man crumpled on the street, running from the law, whose body could not handle the drug dosage sold to him. A recovery agent arrested him an hour before he met his dealer. Now the kid is in jail, thinking about his life.

These are all the unseen victories of bail-bonding and fugitive recovery. These are the crimes that will not happen because the person who would have committed the crime is no longer free to act. They are in jail, arrested by the bail agent after they went on the run in America, or violated their bail bond agreement.

Fugitives on the run pose significantly more risk and have a higher propensity for committing additional crimes than your everyday run-of-the-mill crook. Their victims are the commodities they use for gain. However, once caught, there are no more victims.

A victim will not sit alone listening to a politician on TV talk about the horrors of domestic violence while the man who beat her is free in the state next door. That man was caught by bail enforcement, returned, and is now facing justice.

Other victims of robbery, theft, those who have been cheated and wronged, will have the opportunity to see justice work. Because one bail agent or recovery agent located, arrested, and returned a fugitive running from the law, a victim will know that they are still important, even when the TV is not on.

Critics like to ridicule bail agents and fugitive recovery agents who exact justice by locating and arresting those on the run. They claim it is the bail-bonding agent who got the criminal suspect out of jail in the first place. That statement is true. However, they will not say that their idea of bail reform is to free *all* the inmates and let them run. In their system, if no one goes to court, it is okay. In the program they envision, fugitives can run across the state line and start anew without fear of capture.

That is the difference. Bail reformers would have criminal suspects freed without accountability. Their releases would be based on the *Crime-for-Free* model they love to promote. And when the freed defendant runs, Godspeed! No one is coming for them.

And how does the bail-bonding agent or fugitive recovery agent fit within the realm of law enforcement? All law enforcement efforts cannot keep up nor manage, through investigations and arrests, the number of fugitives on the run. Each week hundreds of criminal suspects are arrested and taken off the streets by bail-bonding agents or fugitive recovery agents. Their arrests prevent crimes. Citizens are not victimized. One scared fugitive is stopped in their tracks to review and renew their life. The courts and the justice system they serve are secured. Families are made whole, as a relief for the safety of their loved one is realized. Stories of ruined lives rebuilt emerge. Lives are changed from fear to hope. That is where the bail-bonding agents and fugitive recovery agents fit in.

As proposed by bail reform advocates, the blanket release of every criminal suspect arrested denies all of these. Bail reform simply advocates the blind freedom of criminal suspects without accountability. Let them run, let them destroy their lives and the lives of others. That is the fruit of the new bail reform.

Those pushing bail reform will use phrases and words that sound noble. They will tout the freeing of thousands of indigent, innocent criminal suspects. They will hype up the greed of bail-bonding agents. They will proudly proclaim how they have lowered a jail's bed count. However, it is the one word they never mention that will echo in the halls of justice. That one word is, **'Victim.'**

Also, bail reform addicts will never mention those indigent criminal suspects released who will step right back into the criminal life that was momentarily interrupted by their arrest.

In New Jersey, using the famous Arnold Foundation algorithm, a computer-driven assessment tool, one-person, Jules Black, obtained his release from jail. A frequent visitor of the county jail after 28 separate arrests, Arnold's computer program offered him freedom once more.

Mr. Blacks' new arrest for possession of a firearm did not signify a risk. After all, how dangerous can a criminal with a gun really be? Right?

However, the murder of Christian Rodgers three days after Mr. Black's release may suggest the algorithm got it wrong again.

As stated by June Rodgers, Christian's mother, on YouTube:

> 'My son had gone to visit his father in New Jersey. And he had gone to the convenience store to get a pack of cigarettes for his father. Well, on the way back, he was confronted by this guy that he knew. The guy said something to him, and then he started shooting out of the car, and my son took off running. The next thing you know, my son is dead. Now they're telling me that this guy was arrested three days before this incident, and he was let out on this new bail reform. It is my opinion that this new system is responsible for my son's death. We need to keep the bail system the way it was because they kept track of these criminals. They have to be held accountable in some kinda way. You cannot just let these people out and let them run rampant through our communities.
>
> I feel responsible to go out and let people know that this system is no good. Do they really think that this is going to stop them from committing other crimes? They have this point

system that's letting these dangerous criminals back out on the streets.

The bail reform system in New Jersey has destroyed our sense of safety. There is no public safety.

These criminals are not being released in Hollywood or Malibu or anything like that. It's our communities, the poor communities. The same communities that you people said that you want to help. You're not helping us. You're killing us.

Please do not let one family—one other family—go through what I had to go through for losing my baby. It's not worth it.

I would like to say to [California] Governor Brown: Please do not pass this bail reform. It is not working at all. And you are going to destroy your entire state.

This could have happened to anyone. Please, mothers, grandmothers, fathers, sisters, brothers, anyone over the age of 18 and your able to vote, please do not let this happen to you. You still have time to do the right thing. So please, please do not accept this bail reform.'

I would recommend going to YouTube and watching this mother's moving expose yourself: New Jersey Resident June Roberts to CA: Don't End Your Bail System.

(Please note that while writing this book and attempting to provide a link to this YouTube expose, search engines will no longer bring it up. Why?)

For information on this case, please refer to the August 1, 2017 story as written in *Courthouse News*, "Murder Victim's Mother Sues Chris Christie over New Jersey Bail Reform." Also, *NJ Spotlight*, August 1, 2017, "Mother of Murder Victim Sues to End NJ's Criminal Justice Reform." The *Washington Post* also reported on this story on August 5, 2017, "Chris Christie claimed a reform was 'good government.' A grieving mother says it killed her son."

June Rodgers pinpointed the key to affluent progressives and their criminal friends who promote bail reform. They are not releasing these criminals into and onto the streets of Malibu or Beverly Hills. They are letting them run free in the most impoverished communities and on main street USA.

And it is the poor communities, often held hostage by ruthless gun-toting gangsters, hustlers, and drug dealers, who threaten them into silence, who suffer the most by bail reform. As their children are gunned down while sitting in their rooms doing homework, dancing in their living room, or walking along the street, it is the people in the lower-income communities who will bear the pain and suffering inflicted on them. As the neighborhood drug dealers destroy their sons' and daughters' futures, their tragic end will not be felt by those living in the comfort of their 40 room mansions or walking the streets of Bellaire.

The communities affected the most by bail reform are first the inner cities. Arnold's neighborhood has nothing to fear, though, as the criminals his algorithm promotes do not roam his streets.

In California, New Jersey, and New York, the politicians claim to care for these impoverished communities, but a simple question begs an answer. Why are cities like Chicago, run by these great politicians for decades, in such a state of decay? Progressive Democrats have run Chicago forever. So why are their poor neighborhoods still the center of crime and destruction? If they have the answers to help and save, why do their citizens suffer more as each day passes? Why are young black children gunned down in their own home, dancing for mom, and no one blinks an eye, no TV outrage exists?

Are Chicago's businesses now up for grabs, with the blessing of those in power, as rioters loot and burn their way from shop to shop?

Are Chicago politicians more concerned with maintaining their power base than with helping their citizens? The power of Chicago politicians is held within the promises they make to the underprivileged and needy each election cycle. However, year after year, there they are still impoverished, still neglected.

San Francisco, which is home to the wealthy and powerful progressive elite, has a homeless problem that is a shame to the world. The beggars and drugged living in feces, needles, and trash are commonplace on every downtown street. Property crime is the new self-employment gig.

Seattle and Portland enjoy riots, violence, looting, and burning.

Why, if all these cities were run so many years by beautiful, thoughtful, and compassionate politicians, are they the centers of destruction, hatred, violence, and despair? If they have all the answers, why aren't their solutions working?

One aspect each of these cities share is Bail Reform. Each of these cities has extreme progressive bail policies that allow criminal suspects their freedom without accountability. Oregon has decided to play a bail bonding agent by requiring defendants to pay 10% of their bail straight to the court. Pay and go, just like 7-11. They take on the role of a bail agent but do not act with a bail bonding agent's resolve and work ethic. They do not secure those who fail to appear in court. They only issue another warrant.

Bail reform lays the foundation for crime and encourages those arrested not to fear jail. It is the first crack in the justice system.

The promotion of Arnold's Algorithm deceives the public into believing that, at last, a foolproof scientific method has been discovered. A computer program that can factually predict a criminal suspect's risk factor for release is here! These risk factors include odds on whether an arrestee will re-offend and whether they are a danger to others or self if released. Like Las Vegas, where they place odds for and against, but the odds always favor the house. Here the odds favor only the criminal.

The New Jersey criminal suspect charged with murdering Mr. Rodgers, who was shot 22 times, was a felon with numerous criminal convictions on his resume. These included: resisting arrest, possession of a firearm, burglary, drug offenses, eluding police, and hindering apprehension. What did the Arnold algorithm see? No algorithm was required. Common sense screamed this man was dangerous and would re-offend.

Bail reform advocates discount this murder. They boast that before the algorithm was employed as the mechanism for release from jail, other cases under the old system also involved instances where the individual on bail then went on to murder. That, however, misses the point. The old system never pretended to be a reader of dark thoughts. Arnold's algorithm fan club touts it as a scientific and accurate reflection of what will be. It is not.

Critics refute bail bonding claims that the Arnold Algorithm is dangerous, stating individuals on cash bail bonds also commit crimes. The difference here is that bail agents do not set bail. Bail Bonding Agents do not arrest a defendant on their original charge, jail the arrestee, or set the bond amount. That process is left with the police and the Courts. However, the Arnold Algorithm claims it can and should be the determining factor in that process. It should not.

The Arnold Algorithm is not a valid indicator of anything except a means to change bail-bonding's power structure by simply freeing everyone arrested.

They claim their algorithm is infallible, a scientific and accurate solution to bail. For Mr. Rodgers, in New Jersey, it was an unfailing ticking time clock, ticking off the seconds to his death. The Arnold Foundation algorithm is no more than a computer guessing game. They toss common sense out of the window in favor of their own gathered statistics, which will never tell the truth of life and death. The algorithm is no more than a computer game of Russian roulette, where no one needs to take any responsibility for the decisions made. The computer did it! The network said to free the criminal suspect.

In New Jersey, June Rodgers' son lost that game. When the trigger was squeezed, he fell dead. The police had to follow the blood trail that led to his lifeless body as he vainly tried to win a race against 22 bullets.

Was it worth it?

And as dangerous criminals are released and individuals fail to appear in court, running free to do as they please, the courts become less of a means to justice and more of just another empty room.

Justice begins with an arrest. After the arrest, the criminal suspect is required to appear in court. If the suspect does not appear, there is no justice. If these individuals can walk or drive across the state line to avoid responsibility for their actions, then it is their actions that rule the day, not the laws that everyone else follows.

And as more legislatures limit the removal of fugitives from their states, aiding and abetting the criminals on the run, their citizens will become the prey and are prey. As these same states cancel commercial bail and refuse to go after the criminal suspects they free, others will suffer. Victims will increase, but unless the cameras are rolling, no one will care.

The false notion that bail reform is reform at all and that it is based on compassion is a lie. Allowing a drug user to continue their usage, so they can die a slow death or OD or go to prison is not compassion.

Love does not free a thief who needs to learn to earn a living rather than steal from someone else.

Allowing freedom to those who live off crime and destruction to continue unchecked is not kindness. Opening the jailhouse doors without accountability is telling everyone, *do what you want, when you want, we don't care.* And many don't.

In a few courtrooms and law enforcement circles, we have watched politicians' mindset and state laws that sanction fugitives rather than allow them **to hope through capture**.

On the run is not the way to peace and fulfillment. However, all captured fugitives gain an opportunity when facing justice. After their arrest, each runner receives a gift. That gift is the pause from a life out of control.

Compassion does not allow a person to destroy their life.

A fugitive stopped in their tracks and forced into court has just received the lifeline they need to pull themselves from deaths' grip. The court they face will determine a punishment, but the court will also open the door to change. It is here, where hope waits. A new future rests in the halls of justice for those forced to face it. They may not take advantage of the opportunity, but at least they are given the moment. They have a pause to consider a future without crime, drugs, and violence. They may not change. However, one thing is almost always inevitable. If they do not appear in court, there will be no change, no hope, and no life.

A bail-bonding agent once arrested a defendant on bond for a bail bond violation. The defendant cursed and swore at the agent as he was being taken to jail. The defendant stated, *"What a greedy bunch of m— f— all bail-bonding agents were. They cared nothing about anything but money."* The agent ignored the defendant's ranting and raving and surrendered him to jail.

A few years passed, and the agent received a phone call from the same defendant he had returned to custody. He wanted to thank the agent who had revoked his bond.

"You know," said the defendant. *"If you hadn't taken me to jail that day, I might be dead right now. But being in jail and being forced to get clean and review my life was the greatest gift anyone ever gave me. And you know, I just wanted to thank you. I've been out of jail for over a year, and I am clean, have a good job, and happy. Thank you for giving me life. Thank you for doing your job."*

In the beginning, when the agent met this man, the defendant had only just started his life of drugs and crime. At their first meeting, the defendant owned a beautiful condo, had a good job, and enjoyed family life. However, within one year, he'd lost it all. Drugs had destroyed him and taken everything from him. Although the bail-bonding agent did not arrest this defendant because he had failed to appear in court, the agent knew this man was continuing his drug usage and living in crime.

For this reason, the agent arrested the man and revoked his bond, putting him back in jail. It was not an arrest of vengeance or need, except perhaps for the defendant's needs who was dying a slow death. The agent, acting in his legal capacity, decided that rather than allow this man to kill himself, he would put him back in jail.

It was because of that arrest and bond-revocation that this man's life finally changed. His phone call explained the changes he had gone through and who he now was.

That is bail bond reform with accountability that does not allow an individual to live in death or destruction. And this is not a lone story; neither does the bail agent involved believe he is a hero nor unique or lives on a pedestal. He just had a job to do and did it. And because he did, a man's life was saved. How many lives will now be lost in New York as their crime for free program releases those who need help, not a quick freedom fix without accountability?

Throughout America, where commercial bail operates, agents work every day to secure the justice system with accountability responsibly. There will always be the bad guy or gal bail agent, but they can be dealt with, have their license revoked, and prosecuted when they are discovered.

It is always unfortunate that rather than discussion, people prefer the sound bites that darken the truth. This writer believes that the best operating principle for bail reform involves both pre-trial release and commercial bail. There are individuals arrested who do not need a bail bond. Where commercial bail has a solid foundation, Pretrial is useful in selecting those individuals who can be released between court dates. However, when Pretrial claims false benefits, they jump across the common sense of accountability.

One Colorado city claimed their Pretrial exceeded the reliability of commercial bail. They came to this conclusion by charting defendants released through their own program and those released on a typical bail bond. They stated their releases were far less likely to re-offend (or perhaps far less likely to get caught during Pre-Trial's timeline for charting crime sprees.) They claimed those they freed also had a better record of appearing in court, thus sparking their conclusion. Their program was superior.

This city then decided that they would take over the release of all jailed defendants because of their great success. And what will the combining of both groups under one control reveal?

The problem here is twofold. First, Pretrial was allowed the pick of the crop. They sorted through the prisoners and chose the low-level offenders, first-time arrestees, and others with a very low-risk factor. Everyone else relied on commercial bail. They then compared the stats they selected to decide the result they desired.

In this situation, their offenders *should* have a higher percentage of appearing in court and include a smaller re-offender group. It doesn't take a rocket scientist to discover that your eating will be more enjoyable if you pick the ripe cherries and leave the bad.

Let's switch and allow the bail agents to select those they wish to bail and leave the others to Pretrial. How will those who push the *Crime-for-Free* bail fair then?

Even allowing Pretrial to combine and control both groups, they should still maintain a better record. They can begin with an advantage. Averaging both groups now would always bring a lower rate of re-offending and okay court attendance. Not because their program is better, but because the law of averages takes effect. The numbers they jumble and juggle can then show anything they like.

However, allow Pretrial and commercial bail the same selections, and the numbers of Pretrial may not look so picture perfect.

When you start with an advantage and use skewed numbers, your conclusion is meaningless. This is only another distorted premise used to pat themselves on the back. This pattern fits others who also use statistics to justify freeing suspects without accountability. They show numbers proving the return rate of released prisoners is high. But here, one must know to what return date are they referring. Many criminals will return to court for the first hearing. Often, they will re-appear for the second as well. It is while the case progresses, they decide that they have had enough. Before they are sentenced, when their fear rises in thoughts of prison or other penalties, it is then they run. PreTrial numbers are also seldom verified. No one else is allowed to open their books.

The second problem with the critics of bail reforms self-boasting is, what do they do with those who fail to appear in court? How many do they go out and find? What is their success rate for arrests? What number of fugitives have they tracked down and removed from the streets, keeping citizens safe and restoring justice for the victims? How many times have they traveled to other jurisdictions to arrest and remove Colorado criminals who are preying on another state's citizens? That number is easy to calculate. It is the number zero.

Bail-bonding agents do not set bail. Neither should algorithms be used as a determiner of granting bail. Judges are fair and better able to determine bail amounts after a hearing. During these hearings, both the district attorney and defense counsel can present any facts and information they deem relevant. If there are cases of need or poverty, most judges are not cold-hearted.

Common sense is far superior to an Arnold Algorithm.

Colorado uses a bond schedule for arrested individuals. This format allows for an immediate posting of a bond based on the seriousness of the offense. If the defendant fails to post bail, he or she will generally appear in court the next day.

In most cases, this is a balanced system. Are there issues? At times, a few judges prefer to give away *Crime-for-Free* bonds, while others can set an exorbitantly high bail. It appears judges go through seasons. Everything operates normally until a judge determines that he is against bail agents posting bail. It does not take much for an arrogant bail-bonding agent to challenge a judge or become rude and negatively affect the outcome for bail setting in any courtroom.

At other times, a judge may decide to set an unattainable bond. A court can order too many conditions of bail, setting the defendant up for failure.

My conclusion is that balance is the key to reform: balance, common sense, and accountability. Also, a help network for those caught up in crime who want to change and end the jail-go-round cycle would be a refreshing addition to the justice system. Those who wish to affect change could set up support networks to help those who do not know how to help themselves.

However, it always begins with the arrestee. An individual who refuses to change and has no fear of the penalties for the offense they choose to commit will not stop, and someone else will suffer.

Where there is overcrowding, inmates unfairly detained, or a broken-down system, the justice department should step in. They can review and make changes.

This book does not pretend to suggest that the justice system is perfect. Just as many criminal suspects game the system, others are falsely charged, framed, set up, and unjustly kept in jail. And when these situations arise, these cases need attention and a fix.

When prosecutors or police frame or withhold evidence that could free a defendant, they should be prosecuted and face the same sentence as the person they attempted to frame. However, we do not terminate the district attorney's office and disband the police force for one or a few acts. We prosecute the offenders.

As for fugitives on the run, someone should always pursue them. A criminal suspect is innocent until proven guilty in a court of law. When that arrestee flees the court's jurisdiction, turning his or her back on the system that promises his or her rights, they are guilty of a crime, and they should lose those rights until their capture.

While on the run, a criminal suspect should not have the right to privacy or the right to hide in another state. They should not be allowed to hurt or rob or continue their life without interruption.

Certainly, the result of bail reform across the country is only higher crime rates and increased violence. And now, as the rioters scream and demand the defunding of police, guess who will be left to rule and enforce justice? Remember the man who dragged an innocent indi-vidual out of his truck, then severely beat him as the crowd cheered. He will be in command.

The rioters who burn and loot will be the ones left standing. Those whose hatred seethes who gunned down more than a few black men during their rampage and violent episodes; these are the ones who will demand control. America should be very afraid.

Within every problem are solutions. However, without an honest re-view and conversation, those solutions remain in the clouds. My goal in writing this book is to remove commercial bail from the shadows. We want the everyday citizen to learn and understand the purpose of commercial bail, its impact on preventing crimes, its ability to hold criminal suspects accountable, and its service to the victims of crimes. We want citizens to know why we believe bail - with accountability - is an essential and viable foundation of the justice system. Rather than chew on sound bites, I hope the reader will begin to see the truth of our occupation and understand the dangers waiting within the shad-ows of bail reform.

On the streets of America, it began with bail reform. Now, as the fires rage, shops are looted, and people murdered, all in the name of Jus-tice, destruction reigns. Their next goal? Defund the police. Is it all madness, or is there a dangerous game plan taking place?

I hope this book shares the truth behind bail reform and gives each reader a clearer understanding of bail itself. Only in an education of reality are the soundbites, name-calling, and lies set aside.

Grace & Peace

www.ingramcontent.com/pod-product-compliance
Lightning Source LLC
Chambersburg PA
CBHW022112280326
41933CB00007B/360